SEWING
dress-up

35 CUTE AND EASY COSTUMES FOR KIDS

SEWING

dress-up

EMMA HARDY

CICO BOOKS

LONDON NEW YORK

This edition published in 2016 by CICO Books
An imprint of Ryland Peters & Small Ltd

20–21 Jockey's Fields
London WC1R 4BW

341 E 116th St
New York, NY 10029

First published in 2010 by CICO Books under the title *Cute and Easy Costumes for Kids*

www.rylandpeters.com

10 9 8 7 6 5 4 3 2 1

Editor: Alison Wormleighton
Design concept: Roger Hammond
Design layout: Louise Leffler
Photographer: Terry Benson
Illustrator: Michael Hill

IMPORTANT, PLEASE READ
Don't mix your measurements—use either inches or metric, but
not both, because the equivalents given are not always exact.

Contents

Introduction

Children love to dress up and use their imaginations to role-play and create wonderful stories. To help them on their way, here you will find 35 dressing-up outfits—something for every occasion.

There are lots of costumes available to buy, but the ones that your children will treasure and remember for years to come are the ones that you made especially for them. This book provides you with a set of basic patterns to enable you to make all of the outfits, with additional patterns for embellishments and extra details to add to specific projects. Simply choose your outfit, locate the pattern pieces, and trace them off.

Each project has a list of materials but many can be adapted using the fabrics and other materials that you have to hand. Detailed step-by-step directions will guide you through each project, and there is also a handy techniques section at the back of the book to help you with the basics.

All of the outfits can be made in less than a day (apart from the Astronaut's helmet, which takes a few days to dry). I have kept things as simple as possible and so have used the minimum number of pattern pieces for each outfit and have made seams quick and easy to do. It is a good idea to use fabrics that do not ravel too much or to cut fabrics with pinking shears, which will reduce raveling.

The patterns for the basic items come in three sizes, while specific measurements are given for other outfits, but I would recommend always measuring your child and adjusting sizes if necessary before cutting your fabric. The fabric quantities given are for the largest pattern size and so you will need slightly less for a smaller size.

I hope that you will feel inspired to use the basic patterns and ideas in this book to create your own designs incorporating your children's favorite fabrics and colors and adding your own personal touches. Children seem to need a steady supply of costumes for school and costume parties, and I hope this book will help at those moments when your child announces that they need an outfit for the very next day!

chapter 1

Animals
AND
Insects

TIP

To decorate
plain sneakers,
cut two 12in
(30cm) lengths
of ribbon and
tie them into
neat bows. Sew
these onto the
top of the
sneakers to add
the finishing
touch to the
Ladybug outfit.

Ladybug

This adorable costume is very easy to put together and can be adapted to make a whole range of bugs. Sew black spots onto red fabric for the ladybug or add yellow stripes onto a black base to make a buzzy bee.

1 Measure and cut out two squares of red fabric, each 23x23in (58x58cm). Draw a 3¼in (8cm) circle on a piece of paper and cut out. Pin this to the black felt and cut out 12 circles (six for the front and six for the back).

2 Pin the felt circles to the right side of both red fabric squares, placing the top and bottom ones 3in (7.5cm) from the top and bottom edges, and the outer spots 4in (10cm) from the side edges. When you are happy with the arrangement, machine stitch in place.

3 Measure 2in (5cm) down from each top corner on both squares of fabric and cut a snip ¾in (2cm) long. Measure 8in (20cm) down from each snip and make another of the same length. These indicate the armholes.

You will need

* 48x24in (120x60cm) red fabric and matching thread
* Paper for patterns
* 28x24in (70x60cm) black felt and matching thread
* 44in (110cm) elastic ¼in (5mm) wide
* Safety pin
* Small patch of Velcro
* Two black pipe cleaners
* Black hairband
* Two wire coat hangers, wire cutters. and jewelry wire
* Pair of sheer black pantyhose
* 27in (68cm) black elastic ¼in (5mm) wide
* 28in (70cm) ribbon
* Black top and black tights or leggings (to complete costume)

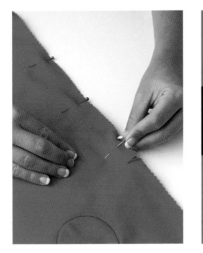

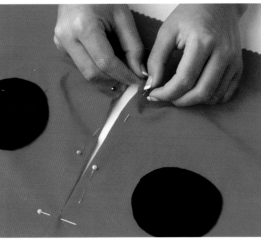

4 With right sides together, pin and stitch the two fabric squares together at the sides above and below the top and bottom snips, using ¾in (2cm) seams. Press the seams open. Turn right side out.

5 Turn under the ¾in (2cm) seam allowances of the armholes. Pin and stitch in place parallel to each armhole opening, and across the top and bottom of each armhole twice, in order to reinforce them. Press.

6 At the top and bottom edges, turn under ¾in (2cm). Pin and stitch in place to create channels, leaving a small opening for the elastic. Cut two pieces of elastic about 22in (55cm) long and thread through the top and bottom channels using a safety pin attached to one end of the elastic. Remove the safety pin, sew the ends of each piece of elastic together, and stitch the opening of each channel closed.

7 Using pattern piece 1, cut out a felt collar. It won't be sewn on, so stitch the two pieces of a Velcro patch to the corners, to the underside of one and to the top of the other.

8 For antennae, cut four ¾in (2cm) circles from felt; sew two over one end of each pipe cleaner; twist the other ends around the hairband. For wings, cut the hook from each coat hanger. Bend the hangers into wing shapes using pattern 38 as a guide. Overlap the base and wrap wire around them to secure, with no sharp ends. Cut the legs from the pantyhose, stretch one leg over each wing, and knot the end. Tie the ends of the elastic together and tie around the center of the wings to form two loops. Tie the ribbon in a bow at the center of the wings.

Dinosaur

This fun costume is as cute as it is simple to make—aspiring paleontologists will go wild for it. Use a romper suit as the base and adorn it with spines and a tail, then embellish with fabric patches. For older children, simply stitch spines onto a T-shirt and sew the tail onto a pair of leggings.

You will need

* Paper for patterns
* 30x20in (75x50cm) gingham fabric and matching thread
* Batting (wadding)
* Fusible web (Bondaweb)
* Scraps of coordinating fabrics for the spots
* Green romper suit (Babygro)
* 43x16in (108x40cm) green cotton jersey fabric and matching thread
* Fiberfill (stuffing)
* Small patch of Velcro

1 Using pattern piece 5, trace and cut out both of the two triangles from paper. Pin these to the gingham fabric and cut out 12 small triangles and 10 large triangles. With right sides together, pin and stitch pairs of triangles together along two sides, using ⅜in (1cm) seams, to make six small and five large spikes. Trim the seam allowances and turn them right side out; press.

2 Trim off ⅜in (1cm) from two sides of each paper triangle. Pin them to the batting (wadding) and cut out six small triangles and five large ones. Insert the batting into the gingham spikes.

3 Using pattern piece 4, trace and cut out each of the three oval spots from paper. Following the manufacturer's directions, iron fusible web (Bondaweb) to the back of the fabric scraps. Draw around the paper ovals, making three of each size. Cut out. Peel off the backing and iron the fabric ovals onto the romper suit in groups of three. Topstitch around the edges (being careful to stitch through only one layer of the romper suit).

5 Using pattern piece 2, cut out two tail pieces from the jersey. Pin and baste one small and two large spikes along one side edge of one tail piece, on the right side, with raw edges even and the corners overlapping.

4 With the romper suit wrong side out, cut a line 10in (25cm) long down the center back, starting just under the neck band. Insert three large spikes into this cut, with raw edges even. With right sides together, pin, baste, and stitch a ¼in (5mm) seam along the cut.

6 Place the other tail piece on top, right side down, and pin and machine stitch a ⅜in (1cm) seam around it, leaving the straight end open. Turn right side out and press.

TIP

If you can't get hold of a colored romper suit and matching stretchy fabric, simply use white ones (perhaps cutting up a plain T-shirt for the helmet) and then dye them at home using a fabric dye suitable for the washing machine. The dyes are available in a range of great colors.

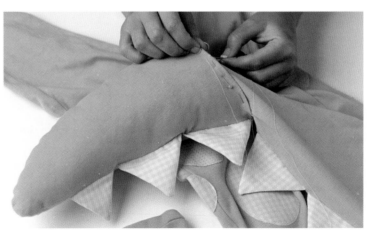

7 Fill the tail with fiberfill (stuffing), making sure it is well stuffed so it will hold its position. Turn under ⅝in (1.5cm) on the raw edges. Securely slipstitch the tail in position below the spikes on the back of the romper suit.

Animals and Insects

8 To make the helmet, cut out two pieces from cotton jersey using pattern piece 3. Place the remaining five small gingham spikes on the right side of one helmet piece as shown, with raw edges even. Pin and baste them in position.

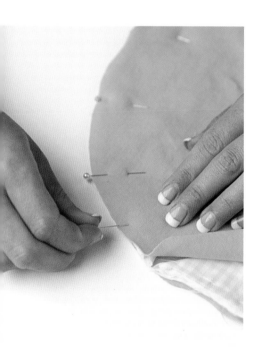

9 Place the second helmet piece on top of the piece used in step 8 with right sides together; pin. Stitch along this curved edge, using a ⅜in (1cm) seam. Snip into the seam allowance on the curves. Turn right side out; press. Turn under ½in (1cm) on the raw edges. Pin and stitch all the way around. Sew the two pieces of a Velcro patch to the ends of the strap, to the underside of one and to the top of the other.

Butterfly

Float gracefully around the yard with this beautiful pair of wings. Use brightly colored felt for a flutteringly fabulous look, adding scraps of fabric and buttons for extra decoration. The markings are attached to the wings with fusible web (Bondaweb), but you could stitch them in place for a more hardwearing pair of wings.

You will need

* 30x50in (80x130cm) solid-color fabric
* Paper for patterns
* Fusible web (Bondaweb)
* Approximately 40x14in (100x35cm) of three or four brightly colored felts
* Scraps of coordinating fabric
* 16 unmatching buttons and thread
* Two 20½in (52cm) pieces of black elastic ¼in (5mm) wide
* 26x22in (65x55cm) batting (wadding)
* Matching embroidery floss and needle
* Two large buttons
* Two thick black pipe cleaners
* Black hairband
* Leggings and T-shirt (to complete costume)

1 Fold the solid-color fabric in half. Pin the straight edge of pattern piece 6 along the fold of the fabric, and cut out. Repeat so that you have two double-wing pieces. Using pattern piece 7, cut out paper patterns for the droplet shapes in three sizes, and use pattern piece 8 to cut out a small circle and a medium-size circle. Following the manufacturer's directions, iron fusible web (Bondaweb) to one side of the felt pieces, and pin the paper droplet shapes to the felt. Cut out so that you have four large droplet shapes, 12 medium droplet shapes, and 16 small ones.

2 Peel the backing from the felt shapes and, on the right side of one wing piece, iron on a large shape near the bottom of a wing and three medium shapes above it. Repeat for the other wing on this piece, and then do the same for the other wing piece. Iron the smaller droplet shapes on top of these. Iron fusible web onto the back of the fabric scraps and cut out circles using the two paper patterns from step 1. Iron the fabric circles onto the felt shapes. Sew buttons onto the circles.

3 On the right side of one wing piece, pin and baste the two pieces of elastic to the center, with the ends at the top and bottom. Place the other wing piece on top, right sides together. Pin and stitch a ⅜in (1cm) seam around the edge, leaving an opening of 6in (15cm) at the bottom. Snip into the seam allowance around the curves. Turn right side out; press. Cut out a piece of batting (wadding) using the inner lines marked on pattern piece 6. Put the batting inside the wings, insuring it's flat. Slipstitch the opening.

Animals and Insects

4 Sew running stitch all the way around the wings a little way in from the edge using embroidery floss. Start and finish with a neat knot at the center so that they will not show when the wings are worn.

TIP

To make the antennae, stitch a large button onto one end of each pipe cleaner. Twist the other ends onto the hair band so that they are firmly held in place.

Reindeer

This is a great last minute costume that can be made in no time at all. A pair of old gloves make instant antlers and, of course, don't forget the red nose, made from a woolly pompom—Rudolph wouldn't be the same without it!

You will need

* 8x6¼ in (20x16cm) beige felt and matching embroidery floss
* 8x6¼ in (20x16cm) batting (wadding)
* Brown hooded top
* Pair of brown gloves and matching embroidery floss
* Fiberfill (stuffing)
* Cardboard
* Red yarn
* 18in (45cm) elastic
* Brown leggings (to complete costume)

1 Using pattern piece 9, cut out a tummy piece from beige felt. Also cut out a piece of batting (wadding), making it ½in (1cm) smaller all the way around. Lay the batting on the right side of the front of the hooded top and pin the felt over it, pinning it to the front only. Hand sew the felt to the front around the edge using running stitch and beige embroidery floss. Start and finish with a knot in the floss on the wrong side of the front.

2 To make the antlers, stuff the gloves with small pieces of fiberfill (stuffing), making sure that there are no lumps and bumps. When the gloves are full, hand sew them onto the hood of the top with running stitch, sewing slightly in from the bottom edge of each glove, using brown embroidery floss. Start and finish with a few small stitches to hold the floss in place, and before you have quite finished check that the antlers stand upright. If they seem a little floppy, stuff the base of each antler with a little more fiberfill.

3 To make the pompom nose, cut out two 2¾in (7cm) circles of cardboard. From each, cut out a ¾in (2cm) central hole. Place the two shapes on top of each other and wrap red yarn around them, pushing it through the central hole. Continue to wrap yarn around the cardboard until the central hole is full. Carefully snip around the outside, slipping the blade of the scissors between the two layers of cardboard.

4 Thread the elastic through the middle of the pompom. Tie a 12in (30cm) length of yarn around the pompom between the two cardboard layers, pulling it firmly and tying a double knot. Cut the cardboard off and trim the pompom neatly. Adjust the fit on the child's head, and tie the ends of the elastic in a knot.

Lion

With just a few "roar" materials you can put together a costume that is sure to bring out the animal instincts in any child. The mane is made by folding lengths of felt and snipping them, then stitching them to a hood, giving a finish that is perfect for the king of the jungle.

You will need

* Three pieces fake suede or fake fur fabric, one 45x44in (114x110cm) for top, one 49x34in (124x85cm) for pants, and one 24x14in (60x35cm) for headdress, and matching thread

* Felt in beige, yellow, and tan

* Fiberfill (stuffing)

* Paper for patterns

* Small patch of Velcro

* Scrap of dark brown felt

* Fabric glue

1 Following the directions on page 122, make a top from fake suede or fur using pattern pieces 75a and 75b. Use pattern piece 50 to cut out a beige felt oval for the tummy; pin to the front. Machine stitch around the edge of the oval.

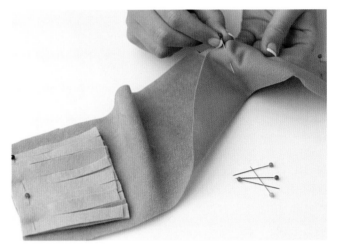

2 Using pattern piece 76, cut out two pant legs from fake suede or fur; join the long edges on each, as directed on page 123, step 1. Cut out a 21x5in (52x13cm) strip of the same fabric for the tail. Cut out a yellow and a beige piece of felt each 4x3½in (10x9cm); make parallel cuts 2¾in (7cm) long in one short edge of each. Pin the pieces, on top of each other, centrally at one end of the tail, on the right side, raw edges even. Fold the tail in half lengthwise, right sides together, and pin and stitch along the long edge and across the end to which the folded-over felt pieces are pinned.

3 Turn the tail right side out and stuff with fiberfill (stuffing) using a knitting needle or similar to push it down to the end.

4 Turn one pant leg right side out. Slip it inside the other leg, right sides together. Insert the tail between the two legs so that the raw end pokes through. Pin and baste in place and machine stitch all the way around the crotch using a ⅜in (1cm) seam. Snip into the seam allowance on the curve and turn right side out. Finish off the pants following step 3 on page 123.

5 To make the headdress, cut out two helmet shapes from fake suede or fur using pattern piece 3. With right sides together, pin and stitch together around the outward-curving edge. Turn right side out; press the seam.

6 Turn under ½in (1cm) along the bottom edge; machine stitch in place. Turn under ½in (1cm) at the ends of the straps and sew the two pieces of a Velcro patch to them, to the underside of one and to the top of the other.

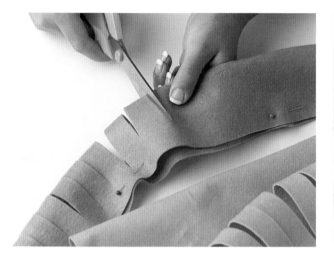

8 Pin the narrow mane piece to the medium one, then to the wide yellow one, with raw edges even. Stitch, using a new machine needle as you will be stitching through six layers.

7 For the mane, measure and cut a strip of tan felt 24x5½in (60x14cm), a beige strip 24x7¼in (60x18cm), and a yellow strip and beige strip each 24x8½in (60x22cm). Fold each in half lengthwise and pin the edges together. Make parallel snips in each folded edge, leaving about ¾in (2cm) uncut. It doesn't matter if they are slightly uneven.

9 Pin and stitch the mane to the front of the headdress on the wrong side. Pin and machine stitch the wide beige mane piece to the right side of the headdress, stitching through all the layers.

10 To make the paws, use pattern piece 51 to cut out four paw pieces from fake suede or fur. Using pattern piece 52, cut out two sets of paw markings from dark brown felt. Glue them to the right sides of two paw pieces, insuring that you make one left and one right paw. Pin the remaining paw pieces to these, right sides together. Stitch a narrow seam all around, leaving the bottom edge unstitched. Turn right side out. Turn under ½in (1cm) on the bottom edge and stitch in place.

TIP

For a fluffier version use fake fur fabric instead of fake suede. Use the patterns to create a range of big cats—for a tiger, for example, choose striped fabric and stitch ears instead of a mane onto the hood. For a leopard, look for fake leopard-fur fabric instead.

Spider

Who says creepy crawly spiders can't be cute? Woolly tights are used for the legs, with a fabric body and helmet with felt antennae to complete the look. Try stripy tights for a colorful costume or make the body from fake fur for a really hairy spider.

You will need

* 46x26in (116x65cm) fabric for the body and matching thread

* 74in (186cm) black elastic ¼in (5mm) wide

* Safety pin

* Four pairs of black wool adult tights

* Fiberfill (stuffing)

* 24x16in (60x40cm) black felt

* Embroidery floss

* 116in (290cm) black ribbon ¼in (5mm) wide

* Black cotton jersey fabric and matching thread

* Small patch of Velcro

* Fabric glue

* Black tights or leggings and black long-sleeved top (to complete costume)

1 To make the body, follow steps 3–6 of the Ladybug (see pages 11–12), using two 23x26in (58x65cm) fabric rectangles. The armholes should be 2in (5cm) from the top and 8in (20cm) long, as for the Ladybug.

2 To make the legs, cut the legs off the tights so that they are about 22in (55cm) long. Stuff them with fiberfill (stuffing), making sure that there are no lumps and bumps.

3 Using pattern piece 10, cut two oval shapes from black felt for the back. Cut two 15in (38cm) lengths of black elastic and tie the ends of each in a knot. Pin these two loops onto one of the felt pieces so that about 2in (5cm) of each piece of elastic is in the position indicated on the pattern piece. Machine stitch this portion of each piece in place.

4 Lay this back piece, elastic-side down, on the work surface and pin four of the legs on top, along one side; stitch. Pin the remaining four legs along the other side of the felt and again machine stitch in place. This can be rather unwieldy, so make sure that you have plenty of space around your sewing machine!

6 Lay the spider flat on the work surface, with the legs evenly spaced. Hand sew a 22in (55cm) ribbon to the back of each of the four legs on one side of the spider, sewing it securely near the end of each leg. Turn both ends of the ribbon under and hand sew for a neat finish. Repeat for the other four legs with a second ribbon.

7 Cut two 30in (75cm) lengths of ribbon and tie one around the top leg on each side of the spider with a firm knot. These will be used to tie the legs to the child's wrists.

5 Pin the other back piece on top and push fiberfill (stuffing) between the layers to pad it slightly. Using embroidery floss, sew running stitch all the way around through all the layers.

8 To make the hat, use pattern piece 3 to cut two pieces from black jersey. With right sides together, pin and stitch them together along the outward-curving edge with a ⅜in (1cm) seam.

9 Turn under ⅜in (1cm) along the raw edges, pin, and machine stitch in place. Turn under the ends of the straps by the same amount and sew the two pieces of a Velcro patch to them, to the underside of one strap and to the top of the other. Turn the hat right side out. Measure and cut two pieces of black felt 3in (7.5cm) square. Apply glue to one side of each and roll them up, holding them in place until the glue dries. (You can wrap rubber bands around them while they are drying if you wish.) Hand sew them onto the top of the hat equidistant from the central seam and about 2in (5cm) from the front edge.

You will need

* 53x41in (132x102cm) fur fabric and matching thread

* 29in (72cm) elastic ⅜in (1cm) wide

* Safety pin

* Two small patches of Velcro

* Pair of black socks

* Fiberfill (stuffing)

* Two 20in (50cm) pieces of brown ribbon 1in (2.5cm) wide

* Black long-sleeved top, leggings, and shoes (to complete costume)

Lamb

This cute lamb costume is easy to make and is the perfect outfit for an Easter egg hunt. The pattern can also be used for other animals, including a dog, rabbit, or mouse. Simply choose an appropriate fabric and change the position and length of the ears.

1 Using pattern piece 14, cut out a front and a back piece from the fur fabric. With right sides together, pin and machine stitch them together down the side edges with ⅜in (1cm) seams. Turn under ¾in (2cm) along the bottom edge. Pin and machine stitch near the raw edge, leaving a small opening. Thread the length of elastic through the channel following the directions on page 122. Stitch the opening closed. Turn right side out.

2 Pin and stitch the two pieces of a Velcro patch to the wrong side of one front strap and to the right side of the corresponding back strap. Do the same on the other shoulder.

3 To make the lamb's head, cut out a front and a back piece from the fur fabric, using pattern pieces 15a and 15b. Cut off the toes of the socks so the socks are about 3½in (9cm) long. Stuff the toes slightly with fiberfill to form the ears. Position the ears on the right side of the back of the head, one at each side, with raw edges even; baste. Lay the front piece right side down on top. Pin and stitch a ⅜in (1cm) seam all the way around. Trim the seam and snip into the seam allowance all the way around it so it will form a nice round shape. Turn right side out.

4 Turn under one end of the lengths of ribbon and pin and machine stitch to one side of the chin section. Repeat to attach the second ribbon to the other side. Trim the other ends of the ribbons neatly.

chapter 2
Adventurers

Pirate

Ahoy there, me hearties! If your child loves to play pirates then get them ready for adventures on the Seven Seas with this pirate outfit. Cut a square of spotty fabric and fold it in half diagonally for a neckerchief to go with the costume.

You will need

* 38x17in (96x44cm) each of fabric and lining for the vest (waistcoat), and matching thread

* 49x24in (124x60cm) fabric for the knickerbockers, and matching thread

* White and black elastic ¼in (5mm) wide and safety pin

* 18x16in (45x40cm) black felt and scraps of white felt for the hat and eye patch

* Black and white thread

* Two small black buttons

* Small patch of Velcro

* Two 28in (71cm) pieces of brown felt 1½in (4cm) wide

* Scrap of yellow felt, and embroidery floss for the belt

* Striped top, white tights, and black shoes (to complete costume)

1 Make the vest (waistcoat) following the directions on page 124. To make the knickerbockers, use pattern piece 76, and follow the directions on page 123 but don't hem the legs. At the bottom of each leg, turn under ¾in (2cm); stitch to form a channel, leaving a small opening. Cut a piece of elastic slightly less than the child's waist measurement, and two pieces slightly less than the child's calf measurement. Thread them through the waist and leg channels using a safety pin (see page 122). Sew the ends of each piece together and stitch the opening closed.

2 To make the hat, cut out a front and a back piece from black felt using pattern pieces 13a and 13b. Cut out a skull and crossbones from white felt using pattern piece 13c. Position them in the center of the front of the hat and hand sew them in place using white thread with running stitch. Sew two buttons on the skull. With wrong sides together, pin and machine stitch the front of the hat to the back around the top and side edges, with a ⅜in (1cm) seam.

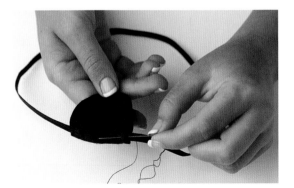

3 To make the eye patch, cut out two felt shapes using pattern piece 11. Pin the ends of a piece of elastic about 18in (45cm) long to one of the felt shapes on the top edge. Check the fit on the child's head, and then stitch the ends in place. Machine stitch the second felt shape on top.

Adventurers
34

4 To make the belt, sew a piece of Velcro to one end of each brown felt strip. Pin them together so the Velcro is on the outside at opposite ends. Hand sew running stitch all the way around using embroidery floss.

5 Cut out two buckle pieces from yellow felt using pattern piece 12; stitch them together. Sew the buckle on top of one end, with the Velcro on the underside.

You will need

* Two pieces white fabric, one 45x44in (114x110cm) for top and one 49x34in (124x85cm) for pants, and matching thread

* Blue and gray ribbons and matching thread

* Velcro, elastic ¼in (5mm) wide, and safety pin

* Scraps of felt and matching threads

* Large balloon

* White glue

* Craft knife

* White and blue water-based paint and paintbrushes

* Pipe insulation

* Silver tape

* White spray paint

* Two large plastic bottles

* Gray plumbing pipe

* Silver posterboard (card)

* White ribbon

* Bottle tops

Astronaut

Blast off on space adventures with this fun outfit. Design your own flags and cut out felt shapes to decorate the shirt then get messy making the papier mâché helmet. Use some pipe insulation for the rim of the helmet, it adds a touch of comfort, too.

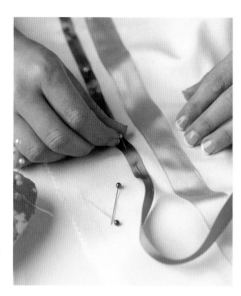

1 From white fabric, cut out two leg pieces using pattern piece 76, and a front and two back pieces for the top using pattern pieces 75a and 75b. For the top, pin and machine stitch the back pieces to the front piece along the top of the arms as shown on page 122, step 1. Pin gray and blue ribbons 1½in (4cm) from the lower edges of the sleeves and on the pant legs 2½in (6cm) from the bottom edge, turning under the ends of the ribbons; machine stitch in place. Continue to make up the pants and top, following the directions on pages 122–123.

2 Using pattern pieces 16–23, cut out flag and planet shapes from felt, then pin and hand sew them onto the top.

3 To make the helmet, blow up the balloon and draw a line around it to mark the bottom edge of the helmet. Tear strips of newspaper. Pour some white glue into a bowl and add a little water until it is the consistency of light cream. Dip the newspaper strips into the diluted glue and paste them onto the balloon down to the pen line, covering it completely. Let it dry and add another layer. Continue to add layers until there are at least four, letting them dry in between each layer. The more layers you add, the stronger the helmet will be.

4 When the newspaper has formed a hard shape, pop the balloon and remove all the bits of it from inside the helmet. With a craft knife, trim around the bottom of the helmet, draw a shape for the face hole, and cut it out.

5 Paint the outside of the helmet white. Let it dry and then paint the inside. (Painting them at the same time could make the papier mâché a little soggy so that the helmet could become misshapen.) Paint a line around the face hole and a rectangle on each side of the helmet with blue paint.

6 Wrap a piece of pipe insulation around the bottom of the helmet. Trim off the excess at the back of the helmet and tape the ends together neatly.

TIP

Collect empty plastic bottles and boxes and design your own backpack, adding bottle tops to make the controls. Try using the molded plastic trays from empty chocolate and cookie boxes, sprayed white, gluing them together and finishing with ribbon to make the straps.

7 To make the backpack, spray paint the bottles, working in a well-ventilated area. Protect all the work surfaces with a covering of newspaper if you wish. Leave them to dry.

8 Push one end of the gray plumbing pipe onto the end of one of the bottles and tape in place. Stick tape around the top and bottom of both of the bottles.

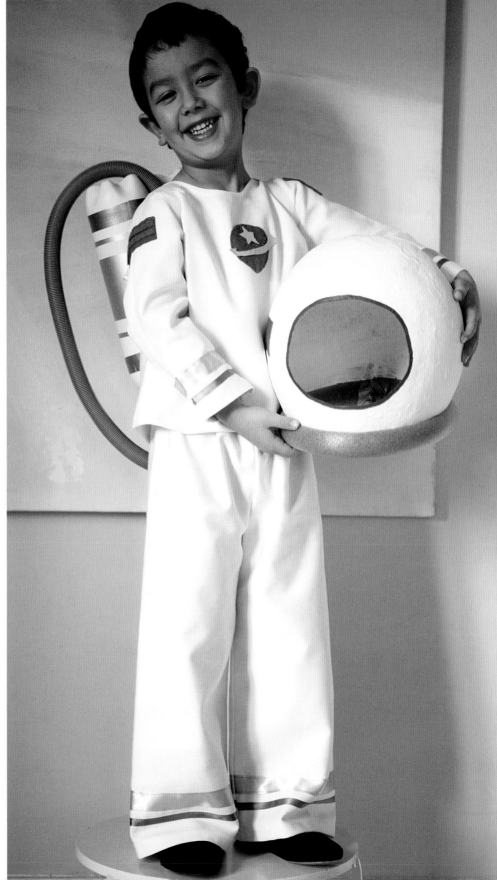

9 Sew Velcro to both ends of both pieces of ribbon. Wrap the posterboard (card) around the bottles, laying the white ribbons inside it before taping the ends of the posterboard together. Tuck the end of the gray pipe down between the bottles and glue it in place. Using white glue, stick bottle tops onto the posterboard to look like controls.

Superhero

Create your own superhero character and make a great cape with matching mask and belt to complete the costume. Choose bright satin fabric for the cape and sew your child's initial or superhero name onto the back for a truly personalized outfit.

You will need

* 41x60in (102x150cm) satin in each of two colors for the cape, and matching thread
* Pencil and string
* Fusible web (Bondaweb)
* Compass
* Scraps of satin (or any fabric) for the monogram
* 52in (130cm) ribbon 1in (2.5cm) wide for the cape
* Two colors of felt for the mask and the belt buckle
* 16in (40cm) elastic ¼in (5mm) wide
* Two 29x3in (74x8cm) strips of satin for the belt
* Small patch of Velcro
* Long-sleeved top and pants or leggings (to complete costume)

2 Place the smaller circle in the middle of the larger circle and iron it on in the same way. Position the circle in the center of the right side of the outer cape, and iron it in place. Zigzag all around the edges. Complete the cape following steps 3–4 on page 125.

1 Cut out two cape pieces, one from each piece of satin, following steps 1 and 2 on page 125. Iron fusible web (Bondaweb) to the back of some scraps of satin that are each at least 11in (28cm) square, following the manufacturer's directions. On the backing paper, use a compass to draw 9in (23cm) and 7½in (19cm) circles; cut out the circles. Draw a large letter freehand (or transfer it from a computer printout) onto the fusible web backing of another satin scrap. Cut out the letter, peel off the backing paper, and position the letter on the right side of the smaller circle. Iron the letter in place following the manufacturer's directions.

3 Using pattern piece 25, cut out an inner and outer mask shape from two colors of felt. Pin the ends of the elastic to the top corners of the mask back. Check the fit on the child, and then stitch. Pin the mask front to the mask back, sandwiching the ends of the elastic between them, and sew all the way around. Also sew around the eyes.

4 To make the belt, pin the strips of satin with right sides together and stitch a ⅜in (1cm) seam down the long sides. Turn right side out and press. Turn in the ends by ⅜in (1cm) and machine stitch in place. Sew the two pieces of a Velcro patch to the ends, to the underside of one and to the top of the other. Cut two 3½in (9cm) circles of felt and cut out a star from a different color using pattern piece 24. Machine stitch the star onto one of the circles and then sew the two circles together. Hand sew these to one end of the belt, sewing through just the back layer of felt so that the stitches will not show from the front.

Knight

The legend of the Knights of the Round Table is as popular with kids as ever, so this medieval costume is sure to get a lot of wear. Why not knight your own child and send them on a dragon-slaying adventure in this outfit? Camelot here they come!

You will need

* 24x16in (60x40cm) red felt
* 49x16in (125x40cm) blue felt
* Paper for pattern
* Scrap of green felt
* Needle and embroidery floss in a different color
* Two small patches of Velcro
* 47x39in (120x100cm) gray cotton jersey and matching thread
* Pencil and long ruler
* Gray long-sleeved top (to complete costume)

I Using pattern piece 26, pin and cut out a single layer of red felt. Fold the blue felt in half crosswise and pin the same pattern piece to it, positioning the top edge along the fold. Cut out the tabard.

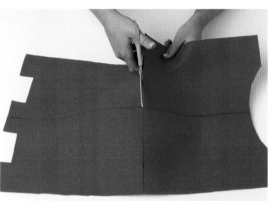

2 Using a pencil and ruler, draw lines dividing the single layer of red felt in half vertically and also horizontally. Cut out to create four pieces. Pin two red pieces to the tabard front and two to the back at diagonally opposite corners.

3 Use running stitch and embroidery floss to sew the red pieces in place around all the edges, starting and finishing with knots on the wrong side of the tabard. Also sew running stitch down the edges of the blue sections to match. Using pattern piece 27, cut out two small shield shapes from green felt. Sew these at center front and center back with running stitch using embroidery floss.

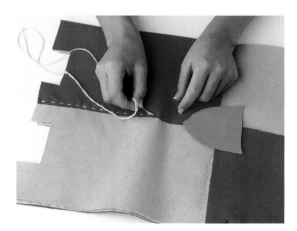

4 For the side tabs, cut two 3x1½in (8x3.5cm) pieces of blue felt. Sew one of the two pieces of a Velcro patch to the end of one felt tab on the right side. Stitch the other end of the felt tab, right side down, to the wrong side of the tabard front at the side edge at waist height. Stitch the corresponding piece of the Velcro patch to the wrong side of the tabard back, at the same height as the felt tab. Repeat with a second Velcro patch and felt tab on the other side edge of the tabard. Use these felt tabs to fasten the front and back together at each side.

5 To make the helmet, cut out two pieces of cotton jersey using pattern piece 28. Right sides together, pin and stitch them together around the head and along the chin section with ⅜in (1cm) seams. Turn under ⅜in (1cm) on all the raw edges. Pin and machine stitch in place. Turn right side out; press.

6 Cut two boot legs and two shoe covers from jersey using pattern pieces 29 and 30. Pin and stitch each boot leg around the top of a shoe cover, right sides together, with a ⅜in (1cm) seam. Press seam open.

7 With right sides together, pin and stitch a ⅜in (1cm) seam along the back edges of each boot and press the seam open. Turn right side out.

TIP

Make a shield and sword from cardboard for the finishing touch. Cut out a simple shield shape and decorate with little circles of posterboard (card)—try using a hole punch and collect the "holes"—and a cross, gluing a strip of cardboard onto the back of the shield to make a handle.

TIP

Choose brightly
colored socks
or tights in the
same color as
the waistcoat.
Team them with
store-bought
black leggings,
shortening
these if
necessary and
sewing a simple
hem around the
bottom. Finish
off with a length
of rickrack
stitched down
the outside of
the legs.

Matador

Olé! Budding bullfighters can't get enough of this classic Spanish costume. The gold braid and rickrack detailing add flamboyance to the vest and the satin cape is perfect for dodging angry bulls.

1 Cut out the main fabric and lining pieces for the vest (waistcoat) using pattern pieces 72 and 73, and stitch the shoulder seams following step 1 on page 124. Pin braid and rickrack around the front and neck edge of the main fabric piece on the right side, about 1in (2.5cm) from the edge. Machine stitch, or hand sew in place with running stitch if the braid you are using is very thick. Follow steps 2–4 on page 124 to finish the vest.

You will need

* 38x22in (96x55cm) each of fabric and lining for the vest (waistcoat), and matching thread
* 40in (100cm) gold braid, and matching thread
* 100in (250cm) gold rickrack
* 16x11in (40x28cm) black felt, and matching thread
* 14in (36cm) elastic ¼in (5mm) wide
* Black leggings
* Pink and orange satin and orange ribbon for cape, and matching thread
* White shirt, colored tights, and black shoes (to complete costume)

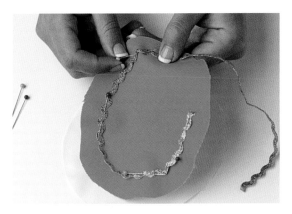

2 Using pattern piece 34, cut out two epaulettes from the main fabric and two from the lining fabric. Pin and stitch rickrack around the main fabric on the right side about 1in (2.5cm) from the edge.

3 Pin and machine stitch the lining piece to the right side of the outer piece of each epaulette, using a ⅜in (1cm) seam and leaving a small opening. Trim the seam allowance to ¼in (5mm) and turn right side out. Hand sew the openings closed and hand sew the epaulettes to the shoulders of the vest, making sure that the stitching does not show on the front.

4 To make the tie, cut out a piece of black felt using pattern piece 35. Tie the ends of the elastic together in a knot. Lay the elastic across the top of the tie and fold the felt over it.

5 Turn the tie over and hand sew the ends together to hold them neatly in place.

6 To decorate the leggings, cut two pieces of rickrack about 1⅝in (4cm) longer than the leggings. Turn under ¾in (2cm) at the end of one piece, and hand sew the rickrack down the outside of one leg using running stitch, turning under the bottom end of the braid as well for a neat finish. Repeat for the other leg.

TIP

For the finishing touch to your matador outfit, make a cape following the directions on page 40, using pink and orange satin and orange ribbon.

7 Using pattern pieces 36a and 36b, cut out a front and back from black felt for the hat. Make a snip where marked, overlap the edges slightly, and stitch to hold in place.

8 Pin the hat front to the hat back around the side and top edges, matching up the edges exactly. Machine stitch a ⅜in (1cm) seam.

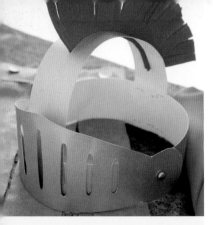

Gladiator

Ancient Rome was known for its brave and noble gladiators so why not create your own version with this outfit that would certainly have made Caesar proud. Fake suede and leather fabrics are available from fabric stores but brown felt will work just as well.

You will need

* 22x33in (55x83cm) fake suede fabric for the outer skirt, and matching thread

* 11 gold buttons

* Velcro

* 24x20in (60x50cm) fake leather fabric for the sandals, and matching thread

* Pen, ruler, and craft knife

* Silver posterboard (card)

* Stapler

* 10x14in (25x35cm) red felt

* White glue

* Two paper fasteners

* 28x34in (70x85cm) red fabric for the cape, and matching thread

* Two 16in (40cm) pieces of red ribbon ⅝in (1.5cm) wide

* 14x40in (35x100cm) white fabric for the underskirt, and matching thread

* Elastic and safety pin

1 Using pattern piece 32, cut out 11 strips of fake suede for the outer skirt. Measure and cut two 26x2in (65x5cm) rectangles of the same fabric for the waistband. Lay one of these waistband pieces right side down on the work surface. Position the strips evenly along this, at right angles to it. Pin and machine stitch them in place.

2 Pin the second waistband piece to the first one with wrong sides together, sandwiching the strips between. Topstitch all the way around the waistband, near the edge. Sew buttons along the waistband, positioning one at the top of each vertical strip. Machine stitch the two pieces of a Velcro patch to the ends of the waistband, to the underside of one and to the top of the other.

3 For each sandal, mark out strips measuring 10½x1¼in (27x3cm), 10x1¼in (25x3cm), and 8¼x1¼in (21x3cm) on the wrong side of the fake leather using a pen and ruler; cut out. Also cut out a 13½x1in (34x2.5cm) strip. Lay this right side down on the work surface. Center the shortest strip right side up ¾in (2cm) from the bottom and at right angles to the strip; pin and stitch in place. Position the middle-sized strip 1in (2.5cm) from the first, pin, and stitch. Position the longest strip 1in (2.5cm) from that, pin, and stitch.

4 Fold the vertical strip over, pin, and topstitch all the way around. Pin and machine stitch the two pieces of a Velcro patch to the right side of one end of each strip and to the wrong side of the other end of each strip.

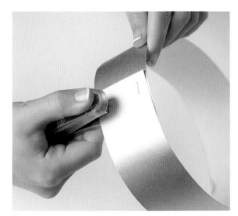

5 To make the helmet, measure and cut a 24x2in (60x5cm) strip of posterboard (card). Fit it around the child's head to check the size, then staple the overlapping ends together.

6 Measure and cut a 15x1½in (38x4cm) strip of posterboard. Mark a line starting 3in (7.5cm) from one end of it and 6¾in (17cm) long. Cut along this line using a craft knife and ruler.

7 Staple this strip onto the headband from step 5. Using pattern piece 33, cut out two pieces of red felt and make snips all the way around them, leaving ⅝in (1.5cm) uncut. To make the crest, insert these felt pieces, one on top of the other, inside the cut along the strip of posterboard, and glue them in place.

TIP

Before cutting out the strips for the sandals, measure around your child's legs to check that they will fit, and then alter the measurements accordingly. To save time, use plain white shorts rather than an underskirt underneath the gladiator skirt.

8 Cut out the front visor from posterboard using pattern piece 31, and attach to the front of the helmet using a paper fastener at each side.

9 To make the cape, press under ⅜in (1cm) all the way around the rectangle of red fabric. Press under another ⅜in (1cm), pin, and machine stitch all the way around. Stitch the two 16in (40cm) lengths of ribbon to the top corners of the cape, folding the ends under for a neat finish.

10 To make the underskirt, fold the white fabric in half crosswise with right sides together. Pin and machine stitch the short edges together with a ⅜in (1cm) seam. Press the seam open. Press under ¾in (2cm) on the top edge and machine stitch to form a channel, leaving a small opening. Cut a piece of elastic slightly less than the child's waist measurement, and thread the elastic through the channel using a safety pin (see page 122). Stitch the ends of the elastic together and sew the opening closed. Hem the lower edge of the underskirt by pressing under ⅜in (1cm) and machine stitching.

chapter 3

Fairy Tales AND Nursery Rhymes

Princess

This princess costume is sure to be a favorite with any little girl who dreams of one day marrying a handsome prince. With delicate detailing in pretty shades of purple and pink, your little princess will look like they've stepped straight out of a fairy tale.

You will need

* White long-sleeved top
* Rickrack in two colors for dress
* Ribbon trim for dress
* Ribbon for bows on dress
* One piece each of organza and lining fabric, each piece cut to a width of 55in (137cm) and to a length of 23in (58cm) for age 2–3, or 24in (60.5cm) for age 4–5, or 25in (63cm) for age 6–7, matching thread, and two 8x27in (20x68cm) pieces of organza for sleeves
* Posterboard (card)
* White glue
* Ribbons, rickracks, and braids for hat
* Two 22in (55cm) pieces of ribbon 1in (2.5cm) wide for ties on hat
* Feather trim

1 Lay the white top on the work surface and cut off the bottom and about a quarter of the sleeves. Pin and stitch rickrack onto the front. Pin and stitch the ribbon trim around the neckline, overlapping the ends slightly at the back of the top. Make three ribbon bows and hand sew them down the center front.

2 For the skirt, fold the organza rectangle in half, right sides together, so the folded piece is 27.5in (68.5cm) wide. Stitch the shorter edges together with a ⅜in (1cm) seam. Repeat for the lining.

3 Sew running stitch all the way around the top of both the organza and the lining skirt pieces. Pull the threads to gather the fabric so that both skirts are the same width as the lower edge of the top. Stretch the top slightly when doing this so that the waist will have a little give. Secure with a few small stitches.

4 Put the lining inside the organza; baste around the top edge of the skirt. Pin, baste, and stitch the lined organza skirt to the top with right sides together and raw edges even. Turn under ⅜in (1cm) on the bottom edges of the organza and the lining, and machine stitch the hems.

TIP

Feather trim finishes the hat off beautifully, but if you can't get hold of any, simply glue pretty braids or ribbon around the lower edge of the hat instead.

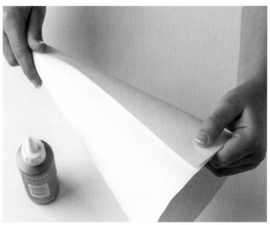

5 Cut two 8x27in (20x68cm) pieces of organza. With right sides together, pin and stitch the short edges together on each. Turn under ⅜in (1cm) on one edge; stitch. Sew running stitch around the other raw edge of each and pull the thread to gather to the same circumference as the sleeve bottom edge.

6 With right sides together and raw edges even, pin and stitch the gathered edge of each organza piece to the lower edge of each sleeve with a ⅜in (1cm) seam. Pin and hand sew rickrack to the sleeves about ¼in (5mm) from these seams, overlapping the ends slightly.

7 Using pattern piece 37, cut out a hat shape from posterboard (card) and one from lining fabric, using the correct lines for each on the pattern. Apply glue along one long edge of the posterboard and stick it to the other side to make a cone shape, overlapping the edges by ⅜in (1cm). Hold it in place until it is firmly stuck.

8 Lay the fabric hat piece on the work surface and baste the ends of about ten lengths of ribbon, rickrack, and braid to the top. With right sides together, stitch the two straight sides of the fabric together with a ⅜in (1cm) seam, making sure that none of the ribbons or braids are caught in the stitching. Press the seam open. Turn right side out.

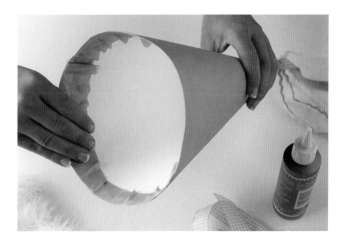

9 Slip the fabric hat over the posterboard hat and glue the fabric inside the hat at the bottom edge. Glue the ends of the lengths of ribbon inside the hat to make ties. Glue feather trim around the base of the hat, overlapping the ends neatly at the back of the hat where the seam is.

Fairy

Every girl needs a fairy dress, and this costume will be adored by all who see it. Simply gather a length of net fabric and sew it onto a pink tank top, adding pretty ribbon roses to decorate. Wire coat hangers are remodeled into wings, with ribbon flowers and bows adding the finishing touch.

You will need

* Two pieces each of sparkly net fabric and lining fabric, each piece cut to a width of 54in (137cm) and a length of 20¼in (51cm) for age 2–3, or 21¼in (53.5cm) for age 4–5, or 22¼in (56cm) for age 6–7, and matching thread

* Tank top

* Ribbon trim

* Ribbons ¾–1½in (2–3.5cm) wide in coordinating colors

* Two wire coat hangers, wire cutters, and jewelry wire

* Sheer pink pantyhose

* String sequins and white glue

* 27in (68cm) white elastic ¼in (5mm) wide

* 28in (70cm) ribbon ¾in (2cm) wide

* Ballet slippers and barrette

1 With right sides together, pin and stitch the two net pieces together along the short edges with ⅜in (1cm) seams to make the skirt. Repeat with the lining pieces.

2 Sew running stitch around the top of both the net skirt and the lining skirt. Pull the threads so that the skirts are gathered up to the same width as the bottom edge of the tank top. Stretch the top slightly as you do this so that the waist will have a little give.

3 With the right side of the lining skirt against the wrong side of the net skirt, pin and baste the skirts together around the top edge. Cut about 5½in (14cm) from the bottom of the tank top. Pin and machine stitch the skirts to the lower edge of the tank top with right sides together and raw edges even. Turn right side out.

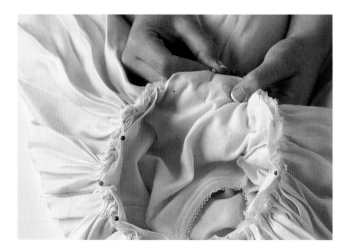

4 Pin and hand sew the ribbon trim over the seam joining the skirt and the tank top, overlapping the ends slightly.

5 To make each ribbon rose, cut a 12in (30cm) length of ribbon. Sew running stitch along one edge and pull the thread to gather it slightly. Coil the ribbon around to form the flower, sewing a few stitches at the base. Fold 22in (55cm) lengths of ribbon in half. Sew the roses onto the dress along the ribbon trim, attaching the folded ends of the ribbons underneath each rose. Tie one ribbon into a bow and sew with a rose to the tank top at center front.

TIP

Make ribbon roses in different sizes and stitch them onto ballet slippers and a plain barrette (hair slide) to complete the fairy costume.

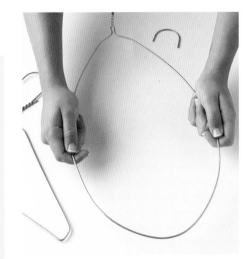

6 To make a base for the wings, cut the hooks from both coat hangers using wire cutters. Bend the hangers into wing shapes using pattern piece 38 as a guide.

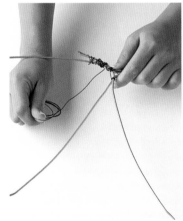

7 Overlap the wings at the base and wrap jewelry wire around them to hold them firmly together. Make sure no sharp ends of wire are sticking out.

8 Cut the legs from the pantyhose, stretch one leg over one wing, and tie a knot in the end. Repeat for the other leg to cover the second wing.

9 Glue string sequins around the edge of the wings on both sides and leave to dry completely. Tie the ends of the elastic together and tie this securely around the center of the wings to form two even loops. Tie the ribbon in a bow around the center of the wings. Sew a rose on top.

Flower Headdress

Little girls will adore this pretty headdress, which is perfect for spring parties. The design is really versatile, too—you can change the color of the felt to match your favorite flower or experiment with different shapes for the petals. Use thick felt so that the petals will stand up well.

You will need

* Paper for patterns
* 30x7in (75x18cm) dark pink thick felt for large petals
* 24x11in (61x26cm) light pink thick felt for smaller petals
* 2x22in (5x56cm) green felt and matching thread
* Two 16in (42cm) pieces of green ribbon, 1in (2.5cm) wide
* Two 2in (5cm) pieces of thin ribbon

2 On each petal, overlap the sides of each slit in the petals and machine stitch across it ¼in (5mm) from the bottom edge to hold it in place.

1 Using pattern pieces 39a and 39b, cut out 11 large petals from the dark pink piece of felt and 11 small petals from the light pink piece of felt. Make a central snip 1¼in (3cm) long at the bottom of each small petal and a snip 1½in (4cm) long in the same place on all the large petals.

3 Measure and cut a 1¼x21¼in (3x54cm) strip of green felt. Lay the large petals along the strip, overlapping it by ⅝in (1.5cm). Pin and baste the petals in place close to the edge.

4 Position the small petals over the large ones, lining up the straight edges, and pin and baste in place.

Fairy Tales and Nursery Rhymes

5 Pin the two lengths of green ribbon to the ends of the green felt. Machine stitch in place.

6 Fold the green felt over so it covers the basted edges of the petals. Pin and machine stitch all the way along. Hand sew the thin ribbon ends to the wrong side of the headdress at each side of the back, forming loops that can be used to hold the headdress in place with hairclips.

You will need

* 73x53in (185x134cm) red fabric and matching thread

* 73x53in (185x134cm) gingham fabric and matching thread

* Two 24in (60cm) pieces of ribbon

* Jumbo rickrack

Little Red Riding Hood

This cute red cape is perfect for scaring away any wolves lurking in the woods. The gingham lining really makes the cloak stand out, but for a simpler version, miss out the lining and simply hem all the way round the cape and sew ribbons on for the ties.

1 For the cape, use pattern pieces 70 and 71 to cut out one back and two front pieces from red fabric and the same from gingham fabric. With right sides together, pin and machine stitch the red fronts to the red back with ⅜in (1cm) seams and press the seams open. Do the same for the gingham pieces.

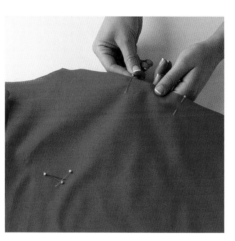

2 Using pattern piece 40, cut out one hood piece from red fabric and one from gingham. Fold the red fabric in half with right sides together, and pin and stitch along the angled edge. Press the seams open. Turn right side out. Repeat for the gingham piece.

3 With right sides together and raw edges even, pin and stitch the lower edge of the red hood to the top edge of the red cape. Repeat for the gingham pieces, leaving an opening of about 5in (12cm) in the seam.

4 Baste the ends of the ribbons to the right side of the red cape at the neck. Pin and baste the rickrack on the right side along the ⅜in (1cm) seamline on the bottom edge of the cape and along the ⅜in (1cm) seamline on the raw edge of the hood. With right sides together, pin and stitch the gingham lining to the red cape all the way around with a ⅜in (1cm) seam. Snip into the seam allowances on the curves. Turn the cape right side out through the opening in the lining. Press. Slipstitch the opening closed.

Angel

Heavens above, this costume is simply adorable! Your little one will look divine in this pretty angel outfit. It's perfect if you need to make a costume for the school nativity play and the basic pattern will work equally well for shepherd and king outfits, too.

You will need

* 52x48in (132x120cm) white fabric for the dress, and matching thread

* Ribbons for the dress, and matching thread

* 26x40in (65x100cm) fusible interfacing

* 26x40in (65x100cm) yellow gingham fabric for the wings, and matching thread

* Fiberfill (stuffing)

* 101in (253cm) yellow ribbon 1in (2.5cm) wide for the wings

* 10in (25cm) square of white felt for the halo

* 2½in (6cm) piece of white elastic ¼in (5mm) wide

1 Make the dress from the white fabric following the directions on page 126 using pattern pieces 74 and 77. Pin and stitch ribbons around the sleeves and bottom of the dress.

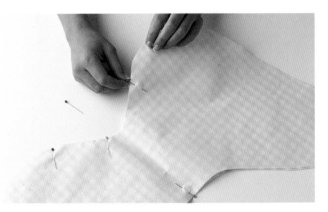

2 Following the manufacturer's directions, iron the interfacing to the wrong side of the gingham fabric. Fold the gingham in half. Using pattern piece 41 and positioning it along the fold of the fabric, cut out two double-wing pieces. With right sides together, pin and machine stitch the two wing pieces together with a ⅜in (1cm) seam, leaving an opening of about 4in (10cm) at the bottom edge. Trim the seam allowance and snip into the seam allowances around the curves. Turn right side out and press.

3 Stuff the wings with fiberfill (stuffing) and slipstitch the opening closed. Sew a 5in (12.5cm) loop of yellow ribbon to the back of the wings at center bottom. Sew the ends of two 48in (120cm) lengths of yellow ribbon to the back of the wings near the top edge, about 2in (5cm) either side of the center, folding the ends under neatly before sewing in place.

4 Using pattern piece 42, cut out a halo from white felt. Pin the small piece of elastic to the ends of the halo, with the ends of the elastic overlapping the ends of the halo. Try it on the child's head to check the size, and then machine stitch the ends of the elastic in place.

TIP

If you are using a lightweight fabric like gingham, it is a good idea to use fusible interfacing to give the wings a smoother finish, but heavier-weight fabrics probably won't need this.

Elf

Create a cute elf outfit complete with a pointy hat and a funny false beard. This is a great last-minute outfit and for even speedier results make the hat and whiskers then team them with a store-bought shirt and pants tucked into a pair of shiny boots.

You will need

* 45x44in (114x110cm) bright-colored fabric for the top, and matching thread

* 49x34in (124x85cm) striped fabric for the pants, and matching thread

* Velcro

* Elastic ¼in (5mm) wide

* Safety pin

* 21x15in (55x40cm) red felt and matching thread

* 10x9in (26x23cm) fake fur

* 30x6in (80x15cm) brown felt and 4x6in (10x15cm) yellow felt

* Embroidery floss and needle

* Rubber boots (to complete costume)

1 Using pattern pieces 75a, 75b, and 76, make the top and pants following the directions on pages 122 and 123. To make the hat, cut a piece of red felt using pattern piece 37. Fold the felt in half, right sides together. Pin and stitch together on one edge with a ⅜in (1cm) seam. Turn right side out. Cut the beard using pattern piece 43, and stitch the top edges to the bottom edge of the hat at each side.

2 To make the belt, cut two 28x2in (71x4cm) strips of brown felt. Sew the two pieces of a Velcro patch to one end of each strip on the right side.

3 Pin the strips together so the Velcro is on the outside at opposite ends. Hand sew running stitch all the way around using embroidery floss.

4 Cut out two buckle pieces from yellow felt using pattern piece 12; stitch them together. Sew the buckle on top of one end of the belt, with the Velcro on the underside.

TIP

Why not make a vest to go with the Elf costume? Choose a nice, bright fabric and follow the directions on page 124. To go with it, make a neckerchief by cutting out a 16in (40cm) square of fabric and hemming the raw edges.

Gingerbread Man

Run, run as fast as you can! Try to catch the gingerbread man! Quick and easy to make, this adorable outfit is fun to wear as well. Buy felt on the roll and trim it with jumbo rickrack, felt buttons, and a red ribbon bowtie to make a delicious costume.

You will need

* 100in (2.5m) brown felt and matching thread
* 26in (65cm) ribbon 1½in (4cm) wide
* Scrap of black felt
* White embroidery floss and needle
* 18in (45cm) strip of Velcro
* 200in (5m) white jumbo rickrack
* High-tack craft glue

1 Cut out and combine pattern pieces 69a and 69b to make one large pattern piece. Use it to cut out two gingerbread man shapes, cutting out a circle for the face in one, which will be the front. Tie the ribbon into a bow and sew it onto the front to make the bow tie. Cut out three 2½in (6cm) circles of black felt and sew each one onto the front with a single cross stitch using the embroidery floss, starting and finishing with a knot on the wrong side of the brown felt.

2 Wrong sides together, pin and machine stitch the front to the back with ⅜in (1cm) seams around the head, arms, and outside of the legs, leaving the hands, feet, and inner legs open.

3 Pin and stitch Velcro strips along the inside of the legs and across the crotch, sewing one of the two pieces of each Velcro strip to the inside of the front and the corresponding piece of each strip to the inside of the back.

4 Glue rickrack all around the edge of the gingerbread man, on top of the stitching where applicable. Curve it neatly around the head, hands, and feet, making sure it is well stuck and overlapping the ends slightly to finish.

TIP

For the costume to fit smaller children, shorten the arms and legs slightly on the pattern, and then continue to make the gingerbread man following the steps here.

Cupcake

Birthday parties are packed with cupcakes, but it's not often you see one this big! A basic felt cape forms the cake, which is decorated with white felt and button sprinkles. Finish with a cherry hat to make an outfit that looks good enough to eat.

You will need

* 40x13in (100x33cm) plastic craft sheet
* White tape
* Craft knife
* Two 32in (80cm) pieces of ribbon
* 40x14in (100x35cm) gingham fabric
* High-tack craft glue
* Brown felt
* White felt
* White rickrack and matching thread
* Pink rickrack and matching thread
* Strip of Velcro
* Selection of colored buttons
* Red felt and matching thread

1 Bend the piece of plastic into a cylinder shape, overlapping the ends by 2in (5cm); tape together.

2 At the front, use a craft knife to cut two slits 1½in (4cm) from the top and 6in (15cm) apart. Cut another two slits the same distance apart at the back. Thread the ends of one ribbon through the front pair of slits to form a strap, tying knots in the ends of the ribbon on the inside. Repeat for the other ribbon and pair of slits.

3 Wrap the gingham around the plastic and glue in place. Fold the edge of the fabric over to the wrong side at the top and bottom for a neat finish, gluing it firmly in place on the inside of the plastic. Glue white rickrack to the outside around the bottom.

4 Using pattern piece 45, cut out the cake piece from brown felt and the frosting piece from white felt. Center the frosting on the cake, and pin and stitch rickrack around the neck about ¾in (2cm) from the edge. Stitch the two pieces of the Velcro strip along the back edges, one to the outside and the other to the underside. Stitch pink rickrack around the bottom of the cake.

5 Sew buttons at random intervals onto the frosting to decorate the costume.

TIP

The cup is made from a sheet of plastic (available from good craft stores), which holds its shape well and does not wrinkle. However, if you can't get hold of any, use flexible posterboard (card) instead.

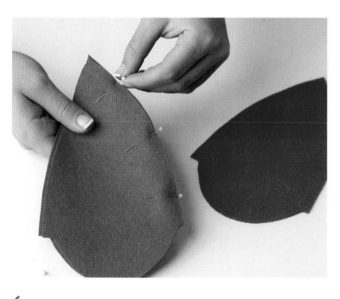

6 To make the cherry hat, cut six pieces of red felt using pattern piece 44. Right sides together, pin and stitch three of the pieces together using ⅜in (1cm) seams. Repeat for the other three pieces.

7 Right sides together, pin and stitch both hat sections together. Turn right side out.

chapter 4

Costume
Classics

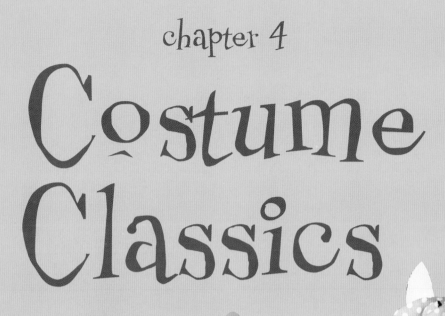

Cowboy and Horse

Giddyup and mosey on down to the Wild West because there's a new sheriff in town. Hours of fun are to be had with this horse-and-cowboy combo. And why not make the Native American costume on page 90 so that friends can join in the fun?

You will need

* 38x17in (96x44cm) each of corduroy and lining for the vest (waistcoat), and matching thread

* Two 5½x3in (14x7cm) pieces of fake suede or felt, for the fringe

* Brown and beige felt for the hat and belt

* Brown embroidery floss and needle

* Gold felt for the badge and buckle, and matching thread

* Five small buttons and safety pin

* Three cardboard boxes, approximately 24x13x10in (60x33x25cm) for the body, 7x7x8½in (18x18x21.5cm) for the neck, and 12x7x5in (30x18x12.5cm) for head

* Craft knife and metal ruler

* White glue and tape

* White and brown water-based paints and paintbrush

* Scraps of fabric

* Two buttons

* Two 34in (85cm) pieces of ribbon 1½in (4cm) wide

* Jeans, neckerchief, and shirt (to complete costume)

1 Cut out the vest (waistcoat) using pattern pieces 72 and 73 and make it up following the directions on page 124. For the fringe, make 2in (5cm) snips all along both fake suede or felt pieces. Pin, then stitch the fringe onto the front of the vest.

2 For the hat, cut a 22¾x3in (57.5x7.5cm) strip of brown felt for the sides and a 22¾x1¼in (57.5x3cm) strip of beige felt for the band. Overlap the short edges of the brown strip by ⅜in (1cm), and use running stitch to sew them together.

3 Using pattern pieces 46 and 47, cut the hat brim and top from brown felt. Sew the brim to the bottom of the sides using overhand stitch and embroidery floss. Wrap the beige band around the sides, overlapping the ends by ⅜in (1cm) and holding it in place with a few small stitches.

4 Pin and sew the top of the hat to the sides using overhand stitch.

5 For the badge, cut out two stars from gold felt using pattern piece 48. Sew them together with running stitch, and sew a button onto each point. Sew a safety pin to the back of the badge.

6 To make the horse, cut the top off the largest box, and in the bottom (near one end) cut a hole large enough for the child to fit through. Turn it upside down so the hole is on top. On the medium box cut one side so it's 2in (5cm) shorter than the opposite side, and cut a 2in (5cm) triangle off the top of each adjacent side; turn it upside down and glue and tape it to the large box. Glue the small box upside down on the medium box. Cut two ears from cardboard scraps and glue them to the top of the small box.

7 Paint the whole horse with white paint, and leave until the paint is dry.

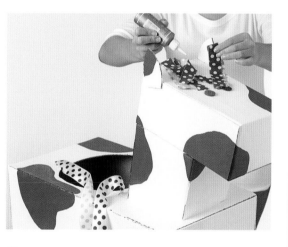

TIP

To make the horse, ask your local stores to put aside empty boxes for you. The measurements given here are just a guide—use any boxes of a similar size that you can find!

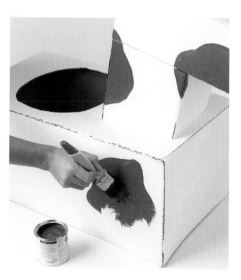

8 Paint brown splodges on the horse to make the markings.

9 Tear 1¼x14in (3x35cm) strips of fabric for the mane, and 1¼x16in (3x40cm) strips for the tail. Cut a slit in the body and push the tail strips through it, taping them in place inside the horse. Cut four slits for the straps 2in (5cm) outside the hole in the top of the body. Thread the ends of the two ribbons through them, so one ribbon is at each side of the hole. Secure them in place with knots on the inside. Glue button eyes onto the top of the head. Glue the strips for the mane in place.

Robot

Transform old cardboard boxes into a fun robot costume, which looks great and won't cost you a penny. Save bottle tops, jar lids, and cardboard, then let your child design and make the control pad. This robot has a removable head that slots onto the body to make it easy to put on and take off, so even robots can enjoy the party food.

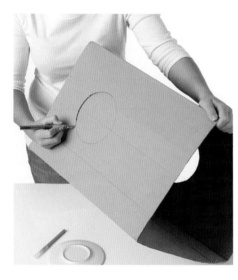

1 Cut off the tops of the boxes and turn the boxes upside down. Using a saucer or small plate, draw 4in (10cm) circles for the armholes on opposite sides of the large box, positioning each circle centrally and about 3½in (9cm) from the top. Cut out with a craft knife.

2 Place the head box in the middle of the top of the body, draw around it, then remove it. Along the left and right sides of the outline just drawn, starting at the corners, cut out two slits 2½in (6cm) long and ⅛in (3mm) thick. Draw a line 1in (2.5cm) inside each of the two lines with slits. Cut out the resulting rectangle.

3 At the lower edge of the head front and back, cut off 1⅝in (4cm). On the lower edge of both sides, cut out a central rectangle 1⅝in (4cm) deep and as wide as the distance between the slits on the body. On the head front, cut two circles for the eyes about 1¾in (4.5cm) apart and 3¼in (8cm) from the top.

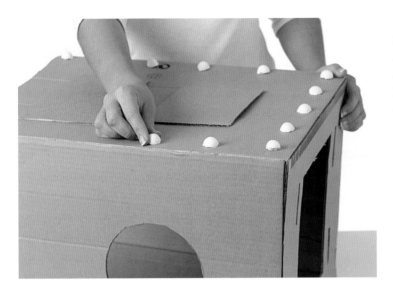

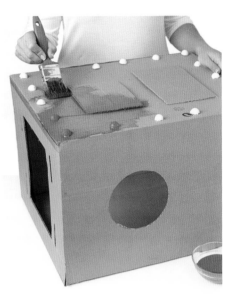

5 Paint the body and the head. If the first coat looks patchy, apply a second coat after the first has dried. Leave to dry completely.

4 Cut out and glue two rectangles of cardboard to the front of the body. Cut the cotton balls in half using a craft knife or sharp scissors. On all four sides of the body, glue 18 around the edges. Also glue one near each corner of all four sides of the head, to look like rivets. Leave to dry.

6 For the control panels, glue plastic bottle tops and colored-paper shapes onto the rectangles on the front of the body. Glue colored paper on the head to form the mouth.

7 Make a small hole in a plastic jar lid and thread the two pipe cleaners through it. Secure the ends with tape on the underside. Thread cotton balls on to the other ends and secure with a dab of glue. Glue the lid to the top of the head. Glue plastic bottle tops on top of plastic jar lids, and glue these to the sides of the head.

You will need

* 59x44in (150x110cm) striped fabric for the dress, and matching thread

* Elastic ¼in (5mm) wide

* Pinking shears

* 18x25in (45x65cm) white fabric for the apron and hat, and matching thread

* 16in (40cm) white ribbon 1in (2.5cm) wide

* Two 56in (140cm) pieces of white ribbon 1½in (4cm) wide

* Red felt, and matching thread

* 40x36in (100x92cm) red fabric for the cape, and matching thread

Nurse

Have the bandages ready and nurse your teddies back to health with this classic costume. Make an apron and hat adorned with a red cross, and use the basic top pattern, extended at the bottom, to make a stripy dress, finishing with a red cape.

1 Using pattern pieces 75a and 75b and following the directions on page 126, cut out and make up the dress in the striped fabric. For the apron, use pinking shears to cut out two pieces of white fabric, one 16x15in (40x38cm) for the skirt and one 9x8½in (23x22cm) for the bib. Press under ⅜in (1cm) on two long edges and one short edge of each; pin and stitch. Pin and stitch the ends of the narrower ribbon to the hemmed corners of the bib on the wrong side to make the neck loop.

3 Pin the second piece of ribbon over the first, baste, and topstitch all the way around. Using pattern piece 49, cut out two red felt crosses. Stitch one to the center of the bib.

2 Sew running stitch along the raw edge of the bigger rectangle and gather slightly so that it is about 8in (20cm) wide. Secure with a few small stitches. Lay one piece of the wider ribbon on the work surface. Center the gathered edge of the skirt, right side up, on the ribbon, overlapping the bottom edge of the ribbon by ⅜in (1.5cm). Pin and baste. With the bib right side up, center the bottom (raw) edge between the ends of the ribbon, with the edge overlapping the top edge of the ribbon by ⅜in (1.5cm). Pin and baste.

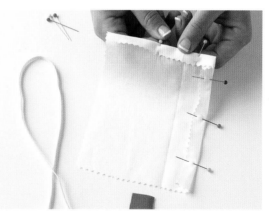

4 To make the hat, cut a 6x5in (16x13cm) rectangle of the white fabric with pinking shears. Press under ⅜in (1cm) all the way around; pin and stitch. Cut a 14in (35cm) length of elastic, and machine stitch the ends of the elastic to each end of one long edge of the hat on the wrong side. Sew the other red felt cross onto the center of the hat.

TIP

For the cape, cut out two front pieces and one back piece from red fabric, using pattern pieces 70 and 71. Sew them together following the directions for Little Red Riding Hood's cape on page 67, omitting the rickrack and hemming the edges by turning under ⅜in (1cm) and stitching, instead of sewing a lining in place.

Native American

This outfit, based on traditional Native American dress, is perfect for Wild West activities. Fake suede fabric works well here as it does not fray and gives the costume an authentic look. Try your hand at tracking animals, or if there's an adult nearby you could roast a few marshmallows on a campfire with your friends.

You will need

* Three pieces of fake suede, one 45x44in (114x110cm) for the top, one 49x34in (124x85cm) for the pants, and one 25x1¼in (62x3cm) for the headdress, and matching thread

* Velcro

* 124in (311cm) braid ¾in (2cm) wide

* Two 9x3½in (22x9cm) strips of matching suede

* Elastic ¼in (5mm) wide

* Safety pin

* 29in (72cm) braid ½in (1cm) wide

* Feather

* High-tack craft glue

1 For the top, cut out two backs and a front from fake suede using pattern pieces 75a and 75b. Following the directions on page 122, step 1, join the front to the backs along the tops of the arms. Stitch the wider braid around the sleeves near the lower edge. Cut snips along the suede strips, leaving ⅝in (1.5cm) uncut at the top. Pin them along the underarm edge with raw edges even. Continue to make the top as directed on page 122.

2 Cut out two pant legs using pattern piece 76. Pin and stitch the wider braid around each leg 3in (8cm) from the bottom edge. Make the pants following the directions but without hemming the bottoms of the legs. Make snips from the bottom edge, stopping just short of the braid all the way around the legs.

3 Turning under the ends, pin and stitch the narrower braid to the top, starting and ending each side of the back opening near the neck, going over the shoulders and partway down the front, forming a V-shape at the front.

4 Cut a 25x1¼in (62x3cm) strip of fake suede. Check the fit around your child's head and alter the length if necessary. Pin and stitch a length of the wider braid along it, slipping a feather between the layers. Secure the feather with a dab of glue. Stitch the two pieces of a Velcro patch to the ends of the strip, to the underside of one and to the top of the other.

Hula Girl

Aloha! Surf's up with this Hawaiian hula-girl outfit that's perfect for a day on the beach. Colorful ribbons are used to make the skirt, with a bright felt flower garland and headdress. Look for cheap rolls of ribbon in your local fabric store or, alternatively, try strips of crepe paper and machine stitch them onto a satin ribbon waistband.

You will need

* Ribbons about ⅜–1½in (1–4cm) wide

* Ribbon about 2in (5cm) wide and matching thread

* Elastic ¼in (5mm) wide

* Safety pin

* Three 12in (30cm) squares of felt in different colors

* Ribbon ¼in (5mm) wide

* Two pipe cleaners

* White sleeveless top (to complete outfit)

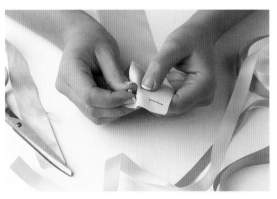

1 Measure and cut 27½in (70cm) lengths of the medium-width ribbons. Also cut a 28½in (72cm) length of the wide ribbon and sew the ends together to form the waistband.

2 Fold the ribbons in half and pin the folded ends to the lower half of the waistband. Machine stitch in place.

3 Fold the top half of the waistband ribbon over so it encloses the folded ends of the ribbon. Pin and machine stitch close to the lower edge of the waistband, leaving a 1in (2.5cm) opening. Thread elastic through the channel using a safety pin (see page 122). Check the length of the elastic around your child's waist, adjusting if necessary. Stitch the ends of the elastic together. Sew the opening closed.

4 Using pattern piece 53, cut out flower shapes from colored felt. Make two small snips near the center of each flower. Cut a 30in (75cm) length of the narrow ribbon for the lei (necklace) and two 12in (30cm) lengths, one for the bracelet and one for the anklet. Thread the flowers onto the ribbons, and tie the ends of each ribbon in a bow. To make the headdress, thread flowers onto two pipe cleaners and twist the ends of the pipe cleaners together. Tie narrow ribbons to it for decoration.

King and Queen

Loyal subjects will bow down when they see this majestic couple. The crown and robe are easy to make and the fake fur detailing gives the finished outfit a regal feel. Extend the pattern pieces to make the longer robes seen here by simply adding extra length to the basic pattern.

You will need

* Velvet: 7x50in (220x128cm) for the king or 138x39in (350x100cm) for the queen, and matching thread

* Fake fur fabric: 29x28in (72x70cm) for the king or 35x6in (90x15cm) for the queen, and matching thread

* Gold rickrack

* Red ribbon

* Gold posterboard (card), high-tack craft glue, and fake jewels for the crown

* 49x24in (124x60cm) plain fabric for the king's knickerbockers, and matching thread

* Elastic ¼in (5mm) wide and safety pin

* Gold felt and sneakers

* 48x52in (120x132cm) satin fabric for the queen's gown, and matching thread

1 For the king's robe, use pattern pieces 70 and 71 to cut out a back and two fronts from the red velvet for the robe and a back and two fronts from the fake fur for the cape, using the correct lines on the pattern pieces. With right sides together, pin and stitch the fronts to the backs for each fabric. Turn right side out.

2 Turn under ½in (1cm) along the front edges; pin and stitch. Pin and stitch gold rickrack ⅝in (1.5cm) along the front edges of the velvet robe. Hem the bottom edge and the neck edge of each fabric in the same way as the front edges. Pin and stitch the end of a length of ribbon to each side at the neck of the velvet robe.

3 Pin and stitch the fur cape to the velvet robe, with the right side of the fur next to the wrong side of the velvet and raw edges even. Flip the fur over and arrange around the velvet robe evenly. (To make the queen's robe, see step 6.)

5 Cut a 22x1¼in (56x3.5cm) strip of fake fur. Apply glue around the bottom of the crown and glue the strip of fur in place, making sure that it is well stuck.

4 To make the crown, cut a posterboard (card) shape using pattern piece 54. Bend it into a circle, overlapping the ends slightly. Secure temporarily with paperclips and check the fit on your child's head. Glue the overlapping ends together.

6 Glue two 22in (56cm) lengths of rickrack around the crown, overlapping the ends slightly at the back. Glue fake jewels at intervals between the two rows of rickrack all the way around the crown. To make the queen's robe, follow step 1 but omit the fur cape. Press under and stitch a ⅜in (1cm) hem around the bottom edge and around the neck, and sew ribbons on for the ties. Cut two strips of fake fur, each 2in (5cm) wide and the length of the robe. Glue them down the front of the robe, positioning the fur over the front edges for a neat finish. Leave to dry completely.

TIP

Make the king's knickerbockers following the directions for the Pirate, step 1 (page 34). For the king's shoes, make buckles from gold felt as for the Pirate's belt (see page 35, step 5) and glue them onto sneakers. Make the queen's gown from satin fabric following the directions for the dress on page 126. Add bows to sneakers to complete the queen's outfit.

Wizard

Alacazam and abracadabra—this outfit will put a spell on any child who sees it. The simple dress pattern is transformed into a striking gown when decorated with spell-binding stars, and a cloak and hat finish the look. Why not add the beard from the Elf on page 70 to make a wise old wizard?

You will need

* 48x52in (115x112cm) satin fabric for the gown, and matching thread

* 18in (45cm) elastic ¼in (5mm) wide

* Safety pin

* 20in (50cm) square of fusible web (Bondaweb)

* 20in (50cm) square of silver fabric for the stars

* Posterboard (card)

* 46x45in (115x112cm) satin fabric for the cloak and hat, and matching thread

* High-tack craft glue

* 60in (150cm) silver ribbon 1⅜in (3.5cm) wide

1 Make the satin gown using pattern pieces 74 and 77 and following the directions for the dress on page 126. Iron fusible web (Bondaweb) onto the back of the silver fabric following the manufacturer's directions. Using pattern piece 48, draw stars on the backing paper and cut out enough stars for the gown and hat. Arrange some on the gown and iron them on, again following the manufacturer's directions.

2 Using pattern piece 37, cut out a hat shape from posterboard (card) and from satin fabric using the correct lines for each on the pattern. Bend the posterboard shape into a cone and glue the straight edges together, overlapping them by ⅜in (1cm). Iron stars onto the right side of the fabric hat shape as before. Right sides together, pin and stitch the straight edges together and trim the seam allowance. Turn right side out and slip this over the posterboard hat. Glue the fabric inside the rim of the hat to form a neat bottom edge.

3 For the cloak, measure and cut a 30x45in (76x112cm) rectangle of satin. Press under ⅜in (1cm) on the two short edges and one long edge, and then press under another ⅜in (1cm). Pin and stitch. Press under ⅜in (1cm) on the remaining raw edge and then another ¾in (2cm). Pin and stitch, forming a channel.

4 For the ties, thread the silver ribbon through the channel using a safety pin. Pull the ribbon through until the neck edge is gathered up and the ends of the ribbon are the same length, for tying in a big bow.

Clown

Have fun clowning around with this great circus-inspired outfit. Choose brightly colored fabric for the top and trousers, then make a funny hat from felt. Add some face paint if you want to jazz up the costume a little more, or use the red pompom nose from the Reindeer on page 21 for a fun finishing touch.

You will need

* Two of pieces fabric, one 45x44in (114x110cm) for the top and one 49x34in (124x85cm) for the pants, and matching thread

* Velcro

* Elastic ¼in (5mm) wide

* Safety pin

* Rickrack in two colors and matching thread

* Red yarn

* Cardboard

* 43x7in (110x17cm) white fabric

* Red felt

1 Make up the top and pants using pattern pieces 75a, 75b, and 76 and following the instructions on pages 122 and 123 up to the hemming point. Press under ⅝in (1.5cm) on the lower edges of the legs and sleeves, leaving a small opening in each. Insert elastic through the channels using a safety pin (see page 122) and stitch the openings closed. Stitch a row of rickrack along the lower edge of the top, and finish both the top and the pants following the directions on pages 122 and 123. Make two pompoms from red yarn (see page 21, steps 3 and 4) and sew them to the top at center front.

2 Right sides together, pin and stitch the short ends of the white rectangle together with a ⅜in (1cm) seam. Press the seam open.

3 Press under ¾in (2cm) on both raw edges; pin and stitch one of them, leaving a small opening. Pin and machine stitch two rows of different-colored rickrack along the other long edge. Using a safety pin, thread a 16in (40cm) piece of elastic through the channel in the edge with the opening. Stitch the ends of the elastic together and sew the opening closed.

4 Cut out a hat from red felt using pattern piece 37. Pin and stitch a row of rickrack around the bottom on the right side. With right sides together, pin and machine stitch the long straight edges together with a ⅜in (1cm) seam. Trim the seam allowance and turn right side out.

TIP

To save time, sew big buttons onto the top instead of making pompoms. Or cut circles of felt like the ones used on the gingerbread man on page 72, and sew each one in place with a cross.

chapter 5

Halloween

TIP

To make the cloak,
follow the directions
for the Wizard's cloak
(page 98), altering the
length if necessary.
Leave the cloak plain
or decorate with star
and moon shapes. For
the shoes, make two
buckles from gold felt
as for the Pirate's belt
(page 35, step 5) and
glue them onto
sneakers to complete
your witchy outfit.

Witch

Whether a child wants to be a good or a wicked witch, this costume is ideal for trick-or-treating. Choose net in spooky colors to make the skirt and team it with stripy tights, adding felt buckles glued onto plain sneakers for a perfect Halloween look.

1 Fold one net piece in half and in half again so it is 55x13in (137x32.5cm). Sew running stitch along the long folded edge (the one with no raw edges). Pull the thread to gather the net to 24in (60cm) wide; check the fit on the child. Repeat for the other piece.

2 Pin and baste the two skirts together along the top. Now pin and stitch the wider ribbon along the top. Fold 12in (30cm) lengths of ribbon in half and sew the folded ends to the ribbon waistband. Cut along the folds at the bottom of the skirt, then cut V-shapes from the net on this edge, cutting each layer separately to make a jagged lower edge.

3 To make the hat, cut out a top and brim from black felt using pattern pieces 37 and 55. Fold the top in half, right sides together, matching the long edges. Pin and machine stitch a ⅜in (1cm) seam down the long edge. Turn right side out.

4 Pin the felt brim to the bottom edge of the hat top. Hand sew all the way around using small, neat overhand stitches. Glue a length of narrow ribbon around the hat to decorate it, overlapping the ends neatly.

You will need

* 52x55in (130x137cm) each of black net and purple net for the skirt, and matching thread

* 51in (127cm) ribbon 1½in (4cm) wide for the skirt waistband

* 82in (205cm) ribbon ¼in (5mm) wide for the skirt

* 22x48in (54x120cm) black felt for the hat

* High-tack craft glue

* 30x45in (76x112cm) black fabric for the cloak

* 60in (150cm) velvet ribbon ¾in (2cm) wide for the cloak

* Scrap of gold felt for buckles on the shoes

* Black sneakers

* Black top and striped leggings, tights, or socks (to complete costume)

Jack-o'-Lantern

Can you possibly say you have seen a jack-o'-lantern as cute as this one? Choose medium- to heavy-weight fabric so that the lantern will hold its shape, then use the design for the face shown here or design your own to create scary and spooky faces to freak out your friends.

You will need

* 48x30in (120x74cm) orange fabric and matching thread

* Scrap of black felt

* 44in (110cm) elastic ¼in (5mm) wide

* Safety pin

* 28x29in (70x72cm) green felt

* Two green jumbo pipe cleaners

* Small patch of Velcro

* Green top, green leggings, and black sneakers (to complete costume)

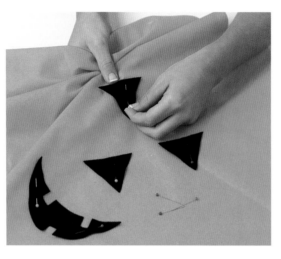

1 Measure and cut out two 23x28in (58x70cm) rectangles of orange fabric. Using pattern pieces 56 and 57, cut out three triangles and a mouth shape from black felt. Pin and stitch them to the middle of one of the orange fabric pieces. Follow steps 3–6 of the Ladybug costume (pages 11–12) to finish the pumpkin.

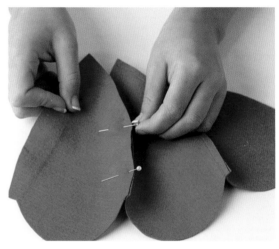

2 Using pattern piece 44, cut out six hat pieces from green felt. Pin and stitch three together along the sides using ¼in (5mm) seams. Repeat with the remaining three pieces.

3 Pin and stitch the two halves of the hat together using ¼in (5mm) seams. Twist the pipe cleaners to look like tendrils and push them through the seam at the top of the hat. Make a few small stitches inside the hat to hold the pipe cleaners in place, and make sure that the ends are bent over so that there are no sharp wires.

4 Using pattern piece 58, cut out a collar shape from green felt. It won't be sewn on, so pin and stitch the two pieces of the Velcro patch to the back corners, to the underside of one and to the top of the other.

TIP

Dress your little pumpkin in green leggings and a plain top to finish the outfit. If you can't get hold of store-bought ones, buy green fabric dye that is suitable for use in the washing machine, and then dye a plain white top and leggings at home.

Alien

Make an alien costume that is out of this world. Kids will love this extra-terrestrial outfit complete with scary papier mâché head and webbed feet and hands. Stick or sew spots of brightly colored felt onto the body and add stripy tights or socks for a crazy costume that will guarantee a terrific trick-or-treating night.

You will need

* Large balloon
* Newspaper and white glue
* Craft knife and cardboard
* Green and white water-based paint and paintbrush
* Three polystyrene balls
* Three pipe cleaners
* Scrap of black felt
* Tape
* 30x46in (75x116cm) green fabric and matching thread
* Scraps of colored felt
* 44in (110cm) elastic ¼in (5mm) wide
* Safety pin
* Scrap of red felt
* Pair of red gloves
* Long-sleeved top and striped tights (to complete costume)

1 Following steps 3–4 for the Astronaut's helmet on pages 37–38, make a basic papier-mâché shape using the balloon. Cut a large mouth shape from the front of the head with a craft knife and paint the whole thing green. Apply a second coat of paint after the first has dried if the first is a little patchy. Leave it until the paint is completely dry.

2 Cut two rows of jagged teeth from cardboard and paint them with white paint. When they are dry, glue them inside the mouth, holding them in place until they are stuck.

3 Push a polystyrene ball onto the end of each pipe cleaner, using a small dab of glue to hold it in place. Glue a small black circle of felt onto each one to make it into an eyeball.

5 Cut out two 30x23in (75x58cm) pieces of green fabric. Cut out ovals or circles of colored felt and pin and stitch them onto the right side of one of the pieces of fabric.

4 Cut three small slits in the top of the head and push the ends of the pipe cleaners through them. Tape the ends of the pipe cleaners to the inside of the head to hold them firmly in place.

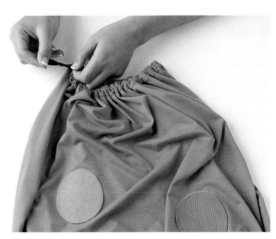

6 Right sides together, make the body as for steps 3–6 of the Ladybug (pages 11–12). This involves sewing the two pieces of green fabric together along the longer edges, creating armholes, and then at the top and bottom making casings through which you thread elastic.

7 Using pattern piece 59, cut out two shoe covers from red felt. Pin and stitch the back edges together with a ⅜in (1cm) seam. Turn right side out.

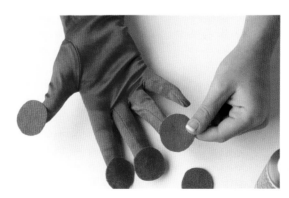

8 Cut ten 1¼in (3cm) circles of red felt. Glue one onto the top of each finger and thumb of the gloves. It may be easier to wear the glove as you do this!

Skeleton

Your child will certainly have a bone to pick with you if you don't make them their very own skeleton outfit. The costume is really quick to make—simply cut out the patterns for the bones and glue them on a black shirt and leggings with fabric glue. Make a spooky felt mask or try using white face paint if you are short of time.

You will need

* 32x18in (80x45cm) thick white felt
* Fabric glue
* Black long-sleeved top and leggings
* Scrap paper
* 16in (40cm) elastic ¼in (5mm) wide
* Black embroidery floss and needle
* Black gloves and shoes (optional—to complete costume)

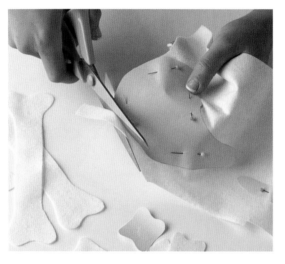

1 Using pattern pieces 63–68, cut out all the skeleton bone pieces from white felt using the photographs opposite as your guide.

2 Glue the felt shapes onto the black clothing, slipping scrap paper inside the top and leggings so that glue does not soak through all the layers. Press the felt shapes down firmly so that they are well stuck.

3 Using pattern piece 62, cut out two mask shapes from felt. Pin one end of the piece of elastic onto each side of one mask shape. Check that it will fit your child, then stitch.

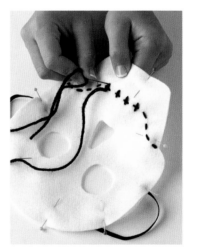

4 Place the second mask shape on the first, sandwiching the ends of the elastic in between. Using the floss, sew them together with running stitch around the edges. Also embroider a mouth using running stitch and cross stitch, finishing with a knot on the wrong side. Sew running stitch around the holes for the eyes and nose.

Black Cat

The ever-faithful black cat is a constant companion of witches, perching gracefully on the end of a broomstick. But don't be deceived by the cute and innocent face—anyone in this costume is ready to cause mischief!

You will need

* 28x20in (70x50cm) black fur fabric and matching thread
* 18x18in (45x45cm) white felt
* Two 20in (51cm) pieces of red ribbon 1in (2.5cm) wide
* Black leggings
* Small patch of Velcro
* Black long-sleeved top and black shoes (to complete costume)

1 Using pattern pieces 15a, 15b, and 60, cut out a front and back for the head and four ear shapes from black fur fabric. With right sides together, pin and stitch two ear shapes together. Repeat for the other two to make two ears. Trim the seam allowances and turn right side out. Cut two white felt triangles using pattern piece 61 and baste one to each fur ear.

2 Lay the back of the head, fur side up, on the work surface and place the ears on it, felt side up, with raw edges even. Baste in position. Place the front of the head on top, right side down. Pin and stitch a ⅜in (1cm) seam around the outside edge, and snip into the seam allowances on the curves. Turn right side out. Stitch an end of each ribbon to the bottom of the head, near the hole for the face, to form the ties.

3 Measure and cut a 22x5in (55x12cm) rectangle of fur fabric. Fold it in half lengthwise and pin and stitch a ⅜in (1cm) seam along the long edge and one end. Trim the seam allowance. Turn right side out, pushing it with a knitting needle or similar if necessary.

4 Pin and stitch the raw end of the tail to the leggings, positioning it just under the waistband. Cut a collar from white felt using pattern piece 1. Because it is not sewn on, stitch the two pieces of a Velcro patch to the corners, to the underside of one and to the top of the other.

TIP

To adapt the costume for other times of year, choose suitable fur fabric and change the ears to make a dog, a mouse, or even a rabbit, sewing a pompom on for the tail.

Frankenstein

He's alive! Ten thousand volts of lightning were needed to bring Frankenstein's monster to life, but you will only need a few cardboard boxes, some fabric, and thread. Practice your scariest monster face before you go out trick-or-treating to guarantee your best candy haul ever.

You will need

* 45x44in (114x110cm) brown fabric for the top, and matching thread

* 49x34in (124x85cm) gray fabric for the pants, and matching thread

* Scraps of fabric for patches

* Pinking shears

* Embroidery floss and needle

* Craft knife

* Cardboard box approx 6½x6½x8in (17x17x20cm) for the head

* Green and brown water-based paint and paintbrush

* Black felt

* High-tack craft glue

* Black marker pen

* Two bottle tops

* Two cardboard boxes for the shoes approx 9x4½x3½in (23x11x9cm)

* Two 28in (70cm) pieces of black cord

1 Make the top and pants using pattern pieces 75a, 75b, and 76 and following the directions on pages 122 and 123. Cut 4in (10cm) squares of assorted fabrics using pinking shears, and stitch them randomly onto the top. Using embroidery floss, make large stitches around them for decoration.

2 Using a craft knife, cut off the top of the box for the head, and turn the box upside down. Cut ear shapes from the sides and a brow from the front. Paint the head green and leave to dry completely.

3 Cut six 6x¾in (15x2cm) strips of black felt and glue them onto the top of the head. Cut out two felt eyebrow shapes and glue them onto the face.

5 Remove the tops from the two boxes for the shoes. Cut an oval about 3½in (9cm) long in each box, about 1¼in (3cm) from the back. Make sure that your child can push their feet through the holes. Paint the shoes brown and leave to dry.

4 Draw a scar on the forehead using a marker pen. Glue bottle tops onto the sides of the head to look like a bolt, holding them in place until they are stuck.

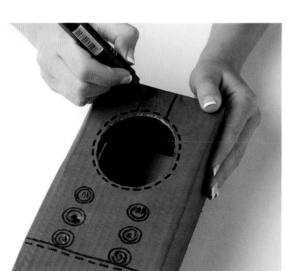

6 Draw stitching and lace holes on the shoes with the marker pen to decorate them.

7 Make small holes for the laces. Thread the lengths of cord through the holes to lace them up. Finish with a bow on each shoe.

TIP

Use old shoeboxes to make Frankenstein's oversize shoes. Or look for empty food boxes in similar sizes, making sure that the boxes are not so big that they could cause accidents!

Techniques

Fabrics

Most of the fabrics used in this book are dressweight cottons, which are available in a wide range of colors and patterns. Fabrics that do not ravel easily are ideal for costume making because you will not have to spend too much time hemming the garments. Felt is great to use as it is easy to sew, does not ravel, and is readily available from good craft stores. However, it is not suitable if you are going to wash the clothes regularly, in which case either substitute another washable fabric for the felt and hem the edges, or remove the felt before machine washing.

Before you cut anything out, always preshrink the fabrics (apart from wool and felt) by prewashing them, without using fabric softeners or conditioners. Dry and iron them before using them.

Working with patterns

The patterns in this book are printed to their actual size on the sheet at the back of the book. To use them, transfer them onto tracing paper or pattern paper, which is available from notions (haberdashery) departments. Trace the pieces in the desired size—the pattern guide shows you which line to follow—and cut them out. It is a good idea to cut out the fabric pieces with pinking shears to prevent the raw edges from raveling. Also, doing this means the edges will need to be turned over only once, not twice. Each pattern piece includes a ⅜in (1cm) seam allowance (the distance from the outer edge to the stitching line).

Lay the pattern on the fabric (folding the fabric first if you need to cut two pieces). Position it on the fold if the pattern tells you to—this will produce one symmetrical piece twice the size of the pattern. Pin the pattern in place and cut around it (drawing around it first if you find it easier). Remember to flip the patterns over for projects that need a left-hand and a right-hand piece. (Cutting it out from folded fabric automatically has this effect.)

To transfer pattern markings onto the fabric, slip a piece of carbon paper between the pattern piece and the wrong side of the fabric, and run over the lines with a tracing wheel (also available from notions departments).

Making a pattern

1 Using a thick black pencil, trace the motif onto tracing paper.

2 Turn the tracing paper over, place it on heavier paper or cardboard, and scribble over your drawn lines to transfer them to the paper.

3 Finally, cut out the shape using scissors or a craft knife on a cutting mat. You can now place the pattern on your chosen fabric and draw around it with tailor's chalk or a fabric marker pencil to transfer the shape to the fabric.

Hand stitches

These are the most common hand stitches used for joining two pieces of fabric together, either temporarily or permanently.

Basting stitch

This stitch is used to hold pieces of fabric temporarily in place until they have been sewn together permanently. Basting stitches are removed once the permanent stitching is complete. It's a good idea to use a contrasting color of thread, so that you can see it easily.

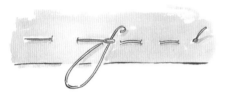

Knot the thread and work a long running stitch (see right) through all layers of fabric.

Slipstitch

This stitch is almost invisible and is an easy method of hemming. It is also used to close openings—for example, when you've left a gap in a seam so that you can turn the garment right side out. It is generally worked from right to left, but it can be worked from left to right if that feels more comfortable.

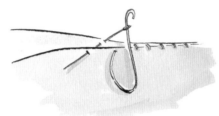

Slide the needle between the two pieces of fabric, bringing it out on the edge of the top fabric so that the knot in the thread is hidden between the two layers. Pick up one or two threads from the base fabric, then bring the needle up a short distance along, on the edge of the top fabric, and pull it through. Repeat as needed.

Running stitch

Running stitch is probably the simplest hand stitch of all. It is often used to gather a strip of fabric into a ruffle, and also for embroidery.

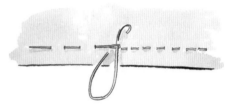

It is worked from right to left, but you can work from left to right if that feels more comfortable. Bring the needle up through the fabric and back down several times, then pull the needle and thread through and repeat, taking care to keep the stitches the same size.

Trimming seams

Once you have sewn two pieces of fabric together, you may need to trim the seam allowancess in order to reduce bulk and help the fabric to lie flat.

At corners, to achieve neat right angles when the item is turned right side out, simply snip diagonally across the seam allowance, making sure you do not cut through the stitching.

Cut small snips in the seam allowances around curved seams to get a neat finish when the garment is turned right side out.

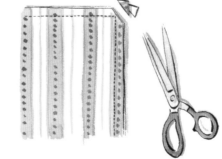
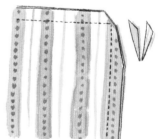

Making an elasticized waistband

Elasticized waistbands are simple to make and are great for children's clothes, as they are easy to put on and take off. The technique can be used for elasticizing cuffs and ankles, too.

1 Turn under the top edge by the width that you would like the waistband to be and stitch in place, leaving a small opening. Topstitching around the top edge as well gives a nice, neat finish.

2 Attach a safety pin to the end of a piece of elastic and thread it through the channel, passing it through the opening in the hem.

3 When the waist is the required size, machine stitch the ends of the elastic together and push them inside the channel. Slipstitch or machine stitch the opening closed.

Costume basics

Many of the costumes in this book include some basic items that are used in a variety of ways. This section explains how to make them.

Basic top

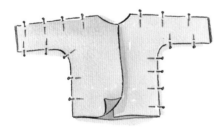 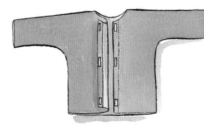 

1 Trace and cut out pattern pieces 75a and 75b and combine them along the marked lines to make one large pattern. Use this to cut out one front and two back pieces from fabric. Right sides together, pin and stitch the back pieces to the front, along the top of the arms, along the underside of the arms, and down the sides, taking ⅜in (1cm) seams. Snip into the seam allowances under the arms. Press the seams open.

2 Turn right side out. Turn under ¾in (2cm) on the back edge of both back pieces. Pin and stitch in place near the raw edge. At the center edges of the top, sew the two pieces of a Velcro patch to the underside of one edge and the outside of the other edge, aligning them so that they are at the same distance from the top on both edges. Repeat at the top and bottom using the above diagram as a guide.

3 Press under ⅜in (1cm) on the bottom edge, the neck edge, and the lower edges of the sleeves. Pin and stitch these hems in place. Press the top.

Basic pants

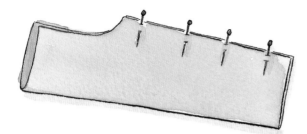

1 Using pattern piece 76, cut out two legs from fabric. With right sides together, pin and stitch the long sides of the leg pieces together on both legs, taking a ⅜in (1cm) seam. Press the seam open.

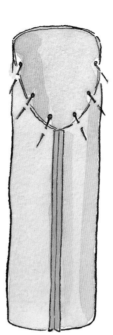

2 Turn one leg right side out and slip it inside the other leg. Line up the seams and pin and stitch a ⅜in (1cm) seam around the tops of the legs. It can be a good idea to sew a second line of stitching to reinforce the seam. Make small snips in the seam allowance around the curve, being careful not to cut through the stitches. Turn the pants right side out and press.

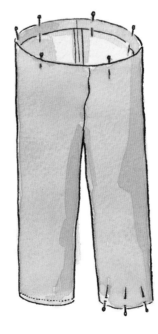

3 Press under ¾in (2cm) at the top edge. Pin and stitch close to the raw edge to make a channel, leaving a small opening in the stitching. Push a piece of elastic through the channel (see page 122) and stitch the opening up. Press under ⅜in (1cm) at the bottom edge of each leg, and pin and stitch these hems in place. Press.

Basic Vest (waistcoat)

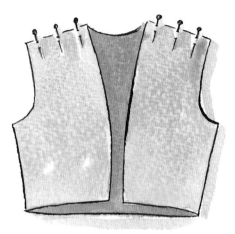

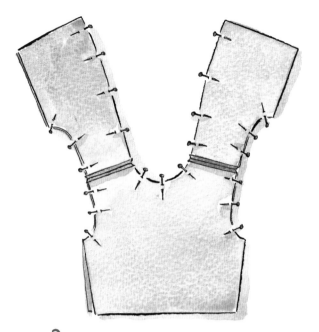

1 Using pattern pieces 72 and 73, cut out one back piece and two front pieces from the main fabric and the same from the lining fabric. With right sides together, pin and machine stitch the front pieces to the back piece at the shoulders for the main fabric, taking ⅜in (1cm) seams. Do the same for the lining fabric. Press the seam open.

2 With right sides together, pin and machine stitch the lining to the main fabric around the neck, down both fronts, and around the armholes, taking ⅜in (1cm) seams. Snip into the seam allowances around the curves so that they lie flat.

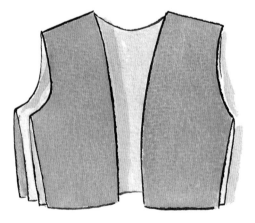

3 Turn right side out by pulling the fronts through the shoulders. Press.

4 With right sides together, pin and machine stitch the main fabric front and back together at the sides, and the same for the lining, taking ⅜in (1cm) seams. With right sides together, pin and stitch a ⅜in (1cm) seam along the bottom edge, leaving an opening of about 3in (7.5cm). Trim the corners. Turn right side out through the opening, press, and slipstitch the opening closed.

Basic cape

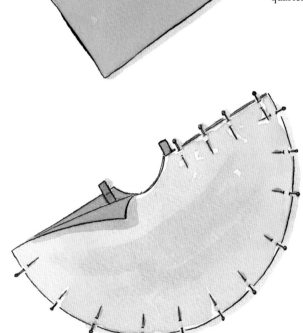

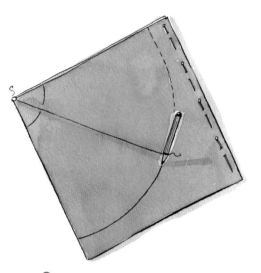

1 Fold the fabric in half crosswise and pin the selvages together. To mark the curved edges, tie a long piece of string to a pen. Also tie a knot 3in (7.5cm) from the pen. Hold the knot at one folded corner of the fabric and draw an arc shape (a quarter-circle) on the fabric.

2 Tie another knot in the string 24in (60cm) from the pen. Hold this knot at the same corner of the fabric and draw another arc on the fabric. Cut out through both layers.

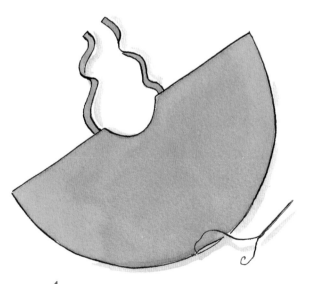

3 Repeat for the lining fabric. Cut two pieces of ribbon and, with raw edges even, baste one end of each to one of the cape pieces ⅜in (1cm) from the neck edge at each side. With right sides together, pin and machine stitch the two cape pieces together, taking a ⅜in (1cm) seam and leaving a 4in (10cm) opening along the bottom edge.

4 Make small snips in the seam allowance around the curves. Turn right side out and slipstitch the opening closed. Press. Topstitch about ⅜in (1cm) from the edge all the way around if you wish.

Basic dress

1 Using pattern pieces 74 and 77, cut out two of each piece from fabric. With right sides together, pin and stitch an arm to a dress piece as indicated, taking a ⅜in (1cm) seam. Repeat to sew the other arm piece to the same dress piece. Make small snips in the seam allowances and press the seams open.

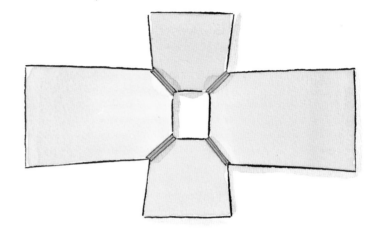

2 Pin and stitch the second dress piece to the arms in the same way.

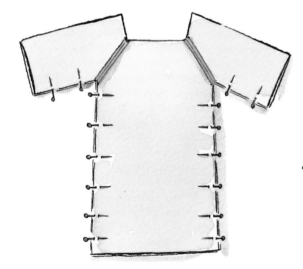

3 With right sides together, pin and stitch ⅜in (1cm) seams on the underside of the arms and down the sides of the dress. Make small snips under the arms and press the seams open.

4 Press under ⅜in (1cm) at the neck edge. Pin and stitch all the way around, leaving a small opening for the elastic. Thread elastic through this channel (see page 122) and stitch the opening closed. Press under ⅜in (1cm) at the bottom edge of the dress and lower edges of the sleeves; pin and stitch.

Suppliers

US Suppliers

A.C. Moore
Stores nationwide
1-888-226-6673
www.acmoore.com

Art Supplies Online
800-363-7709
www.artsuppliesonline.com

Consumer Crafts
1-888-552-7238
www.consumercrafts.com

Craft Site Directory
Useful online resource
www.craftsitedirectory.com

Create For Less
866-333-4463
www.createforless.com

Darice
866-432-7423
www.darice.com

Hobby Lobby
Stores nationwide
www.hobbylobby.com

Jo-Ann Fabric and Craft Store
Stores nationwide
1-888-739-4120
www.joann.com

Kids Craft Supplies
866 777-8654
www.kidscraftsupplies.com

Michaels
Stores nationwide
1-800-642-4235
www.michaels.com

S&S Worldwide Craft Supplies
800-288-9941
www.ssww.com

Toys "R" Us
Stores nationwide
www.toysrus.com

UK Suppliers

Baker Ross
0333 200 7230
bakerross.co.uk

Early Learning Centre
0371 231 3513
www.elc.co.uk

Homecrafts
0116 269 7733
www.homecrafts.co.uk

Hobbycraft
0330 026 1400
www.hobbycraft.co.uk

John Lewis
03456 049 049
www.johnlewis.co.uk

Kidzcraft
01793 327022
www.kidzcraft.co.uk

Paperchase
0161 839 1500
www.paperchase.co.uk

Paper and String
www.paper-and-string.co.uk

Acknowledgments

A huge thank you to Terry Benson for such brilliant photography and for working so hard to get the right shots. And many thanks to Jodie Allen for all the help and assistance and for having lovely hands! You were both a real pleasure to work with.
Thank you to Leonora French for modeling so beautifully. Thank you to Pete Jorgensen for knocking it all into shape and for unstinting help throughout the project, Alison Wormleighton for patient and sensitive editing, Louise Leffler for great design, Sally Powell for organizing lovely models, and Cindy Richards for commissioning me to do the book. And as ever, thank you to Laurie, Gracie, and Betty.

Index